Bluffer's
GUIDE TO
PUBLIC
RELATIONS

KEITH HANN

© Haynes Publishing 2019
Published March 2019

A CIP Catalogue record for this book
is available from the British Library.

ISBN: 978 1 78521 564 3 (print)
      978 1 78521 626 8 (eBook)

Library of Congress control no. 2018967376

Published by Haynes Publishing,
Sparkford, Yeovil, Somerset BA22 7JJ
Tel: 01963 440635
Int. tel: +44 1963 440635
Website: www.haynes.com

Printed in Malaysia.

Bluffer's Guide®, Bluffer's® and Bluff Your Way®
are registered trademarks.

Series Editor: David Allsop.
Front cover illustration by Alan Capel.

CONTENTS

THE FIRST RULE OF PR

This is the most tremendously exciting and fantastically useful book ever published on the subject of public relations in the entire history of human life on Earth.

Actually it isn't, but that is exactly the sort of thing you are going to have to learn to say with a straight face if you have bought or blagged a loan of this copy in the hope of bluffing your way into the world of PR.

By the time you get to the end of it you should have a firm grasp of the essentials, but you should remain conscious at all times of the First Rule of PR.

Which is simply this.

Never believe your own PR.

B̆

'Reputation, reputation, reputation! Oh, I have lost my reputation! I have lost the immortal part of myself, and what remains is bestial.'

William Shakespeare, Othello

THE IMPORTANCE OF REPUTATION

Public relations is all about reputation, whether of an individual, organisation or state (hereinafter called 'the client'): maintaining it and improving it as far as possible, or limiting the damage when it comes under attack. If we accept the verdict of Shakespeare that nothing matters more than reputation, then clearly being a Public Relations person (hereinafter abbreviated for convenience to 'PR') is simply the most important job in the world.

The principles are quite simple. Inform, persuade and engage with the public in the hope of bettering their understanding of the client (or restricting it if the client is, for example, Murder Incorporated). While engaging, take care to listen to the public and do your very best to understand what they are trying to tell you. And at all times, take the utmost care to treat the public the way you would like to be treated yourself.

Put like that, it sounds too easy to be a real job, so the PR will dress it up with a lot of waffle about 'reaching out to stakeholders' and 'building mutually beneficial partnerships'.

And this brings us straight away to the nub of this book. There are many occupations in which it is advantageous to be a bluffer, but PR is surely the only one in which the ability to bluff successfully is widely believed to be the sum total of the job description.

If we accept the verdict of Shakespeare that nothing matters more than reputation, then clearly being a Public Relations person is simply the most important job in the world.

We have all met tradesmen who are clearly bluffing when they claim to know how to fix your plumbing or rescue your sagging gable, as you discover shortly afterwards when you are sitting in the pile of rubble that was once your house, trying to rescue your insurance policy from the rapidly rising waters. But if you ever meet a PR who cannot bluff you have encountered someone who has made a job choice as spectacularly wrong as a vegan working in an abattoir.

And while an incompetently bluffing builder, plumber or electrician may wreck your home, a bluffing mechanic is highly likely to ruin your car, and a bluffing lawyer could easily land you in prison or destitution, a PR who **isn't** a world-class expert in bluffing might well destroy your reputation.

And, as was established right at the outset, there is nothing in this world more important than that.

WHERE DID IT START?

Everything needs a back story in the interests of respectability. A profession can't simply have been invented on a whim by someone in a pub or a yoga class. So the bluffer will point out instead that ancient Babylonian clay tablets are cited as the first instance of PR in action (perhaps the annual report of Hanging Gardens plc). Then there are all those ancient Egyptian obelisks, and what are the pyramids but a fantastic exercise in PR for the pharaohs? (Don't mention this to a 21st century client, though, or they will surely want one.) Plus, of course, that poetic pedestal inscribed 'My name is Ozymandias, King of Kings; Look on my Works, ye Mighty, and despair!' (With that ready-made strapline for the website, the failure to create a firm called Ozymandias Communications has always seemed something of a mystery.)

PR may perhaps have taken a step backwards in ancient Rome, where legend tells us that a slave was placed in the chariots of victorious generals to whisper constantly 'Remember you are mortal' as they enjoyed the adulation of the populace. Whereas any half decent PR would surely have been yelling 'Come on, the people adore you! You should be the emperor! You're going to live forever! You're going to learn how to fly! There's literally nothing you can't do! In fact, I bet you could kill that lion there with your bare hands ... oh Mars and Pluto*, what a mess!'

* BLUFFER'S TIP: *Mars and Pluto were the Roman gods of war and death, and therefore those most likely to be invoked by anyone unfortunate enough to find themselves fighting a lion. Unless they found themselves in that predicament by virtue of being an early Christian.*

But PR was clearly well back in its stride by the close of Europe's Dark Ages. The master bluffer who handled King Alfred's PR has gained him a lasting reputation as a genius for burning some cakes, while the halfwit who advised King Cnut has consigned him to history as a delusional idiot for attempting a perfectly sensible demonstration to his courtiers that he could not, in fact, command the waves. He also lost many additional points for failing to bring in a branding consultant to change the client's name to something far less open to ribald misrepresentation.

Meanwhile, across the North Atlantic Erik the Red, father of the more famous Leif, was pulling off one of the most audacious PR stunts of all time by attracting settlers to some ice-bound wastes by giving them the appealing name of Greenland. (Admittedly Greenland was, by all accounts, rather less ice-bound in 895 AD than it became through the mediaeval and modern periods until global warming kicked in.)

Failure to employ the right PR was clearly central

to the defeat of King Harold II at the Battle of Hastings, after which William I's inspired adviser not only said, 'I think "the Conqueror" has a bit of a ring to it, don't you?' but also suggested a bloody great tapestry to commemorate the event, thereby pocketing a large backhander from his other client, Bayeux Weaving plc.

Richard III and Bloody Mary had lousy PR, while Henry VIII and Elizabeth I were advised by master bluffers, massively incentivised by the probability of literally losing their heads if they put a foot wrong. Some argue that court jesters, with their ability to speak truth to power without (always) being executed, were the true forerunners of today's political special advisers.

The word 'propaganda' was invented by a Pope, no less: Gregory XV, who established the Sacra Congregatio de Propaganda Fide (Sacred Congregation for the Propagation of the Faith) in 1622. But that is only to be expected since God has enjoyed absolutely great PR since Eve plucked that apple from the tree. The devil, on the other hand, is in serious need of a new agency.

Recognisable PR skills were used to tempt colonists to the New World of North and South America, glossing over such little local difficulties as the climate, disease and far from friendly locals. (PRs working for bars in Newcastle upon Tyne in the north of England still use this as their template.)

Coronations were PR events. Battles were PR events. The Boston Tea Party was a PR event. In fact, pretty much everything in history was a PR event, simply because there was a bluffer there to record it and so make it history.

THE PROFESSIONALISATION OF PR

PRs like to pretend that they are pursuing a profession – and, if it is accepted that prostitution qualifies as the oldest one, it must be conceded that they might have a point. Today only pedantic dinosaurs persist in characterising it as a mere trade.

However it is described, PR undoubtedly came to be regarded as a genuine full-time occupation in the early 20th century, and the two men who vie for the credit (or blame) for that are both Americans:

Edward Bernays (1891–1995) set himself up as a 'public relations counsel' in New York in 1919 and ended his implausibly long life dubbed 'the father of public relations' in his *New York Times* obituary. This demonstrated that, if nothing else, he had done a massively successful PR job on his own reputation. A 'double nephew' of Sigmund Freud, he was naturally big on what P.G. Wodehouse called 'the psychology of the individual' and his dubious achievements included persuading more women to smoke (preferably Lucky Strike cigarettes), encouraging Americans to eat cooked breakfasts, and promoting the interests of the United Fruit Company in Guatemala. Josef Goebbels was allegedly a fan of his books. It seems slightly odd, with hindsight, that he did not also claim credit for the invention of the almost eponymous sauce.

Ivy Lee (1877–1934) is called by some 'the founder of modern public relations' and he can certainly claim to have been the first in-house PR with executive status, when he was hired full-time by the Pennsylvania Railroad in 1912. Like Bernays, he set up his own public relations counselling business in 1919, calling it 'Ivy Lee & Associates' and thus setting the benchmark for every one-person PR firm in the history of the world since that date. He is alleged to have said 'Tell the truth, because sooner or later the public will find out anyway. And if the public doesn't like what you are doing, change your policies and bring them into line with what people want.' But he might not have done. He was a PR man, after all, even if he had what many unenlightened types of his day might have considered a girl's name.

WARTIME PROPAGANDA

In public relations as in military technology, the two world wars vastly accelerated development, though the output of the warring states is usually described as propaganda rather than PR. The exact difference between these two disciplines has long been the subject of intense debate, with PR types strangely seeming to favour the conclusion that PR is based firmly on true facts, while the propagandist will happily mobilise any old lie to convince their audience.

Long experience suggests that not all PRs adhere as consistently and scrupulously to the truth as this theoretical dividing line suggests. Nor, at the risk of admitting to some anti-Axis bias, were all wartime propagandists liars. But a good principle for anyone contemplating a career in PR is this: bluff by all means, and at all times; be economical with the actualité if you must; but never, ever tell an outright lie. It is not in your own interests or of those of your client because, as Ivy Lee observed, the truth will always emerge eventually.

THE POST-WAR PR BOOM

Like babies, PR boomed after the Second World War. One of these phenomena was definitely caused by an increase in sexual intercourse. The other almost certainly contributed to it. All those thrown out of work in the propaganda arms of the various participants in the conflict were on the look-out for new and profitable employment, if they weren't behind bars looking for a good lawyer to defend them against charges of war crimes.

And so consulting firms proliferated on both sides of the Atlantic. The still famous (among PR people) American firm of Edelman was founded in 1952, and its rival Burson-Marsteller in 1953.

As in any expanding industry, there also began a quest to be taken seriously and considered respectable. In pursuit of this, the Public Relations Society of America was founded in 1947 and what is now the Chartered Institute of Public Relations in London in 1948. ('Chartered' is the adjective Brits tend to use when they can't quite claim the cachet of 'Royal', though no doubt there are PRs working on that.)

In 1967, when a journalist called Nesta Hollis had the brainwave of launching a Press & PR Annual in the UK, it was a small booklet listing just 46 PR firms. By 1996 it had grown to 1,000 pages and by 2013 the ActiMedia PR database recorded that there were no fewer than 4,200 PR firms operating in the country.

THE 1980S

The 1980s was the decade when everything changed and UK PR consultancy really took off, driven by radical developments in both politics and technology. The election of Margaret Thatcher in 1979 ended the UK's cosy post-war political consensus and created a huge new demand for PR specialists, not least to transform the images of dozy nationalised monopolies and facilitate their sale to the unsuspecting citizens who, as taxpayers, theoretically owned them already.

In January 1986 Rupert Murdoch moved production of his newspapers to Wapping in east London, ultimately breaking the power of the British print unions, while in October of the same year 'Big Bang' in the City of London smashed up the long-established gentlemanly cartel of traditional merchant banks and stockbroking and jobbing partnerships. This ushered in a brave new world of international investment banks and computerised global capitalism. All these new 'greed is good' entities were active users of PR – as were the many emerging fashion, food and other consumer goods companies emerging to exploit the new 'Loadsamoney' culture. This was the golden age of the type of consumer agency memorably parodied in the British sitcom *Absolutely Fabulous*: a world of chain smoking, heavy drinking, brick-sized first generation mobile phones and constantly whirring fax machines.

Meanwhile, the transatlantic partnership of Reagan and Thatcher was bringing the Cold War with the USSR to a victorious conclusion, and Tim Berners-Lee was coming up with a bright idea called the World Wide Web (almost certainly the only invention in history whose initials contain more syllables than its full name).

THE 21st CENTURY

Shortly after the British press deserted its traditional base in Fleet Street, the growing power of the internet systematically sucked money out of newspaper publishing and much of the fun out of being a journalist. Declining sales and contracting advertising revenues naturally developed into a drive to cut costs, resulting in regular calls for volunteers to be made redundant – a temptation no doubt massively increased by the fact that a job that had once involved sobering up enough to write some copy for a single evening deadline (and only being sober once a week in the case of Sunday journalists) now involved churning out constant verbiage for rolling website updates.

Small wonder, then, that PR waxed ever fatter as the traditional mainstream media shrank. By 2014 the US Department of Labor was reporting that PRs outnumbered journalists there by 4.6 to 1. Unsurprisingly, given that PRs earned, on average, 50% more than hacks. In the UK the 2016 PR Census calculated the ratio as a rather less alarming 1.3 to 1 in favour of the PR community.

Clearly, if these trends are extrapolated, by the end of the present century the relationship between PRs and journalists will resemble nothing so much as that between humanity and the great apes. PRs will wring their hands about the endangered species in much the same way that the caring sections of society fret about the fate of the orang-utan. And the world as a whole will be poorer if, without the moderating and questioning influence of the press, PRs are simply let loose to spin upon the general public.

WHO WORKS IN PR?

The glib answer here is clearly 'no one'. Everyone employed in public relations is having so much fun that it could surely never be categorised as 'work' in the normal sense of the word.

So consider instead the sort of people who are **employed** in PR.

EX-HACKS

Traditionally, the main highway into PR was that of the poacher turned gamekeeper: the fearless investigative hack who realised that life might be equally bibulous, considerably better rewarded and somewhat less demanding on what many still refer to as 'the dark side'.

Journalists naturally believe that they start in PR with one huge inbuilt advantage: they know exactly what constitutes a story. Sadly, they are destined to spend much of their working lives at the beck and call of clients who haven't a clue what constitutes a story but know that they are paying good money to read about themselves and their organisations in the papers, or even better see them on TV, and expect to do so regardless of whether they are interesting or not. Added to which, there is the regular frustration of being presented with an absolutely corking story that your client is prepared to pay handsomely to keep **OUT** of the news.

The hidden output of PR may not quite assume iceberg proportions, but in many cases success will definitely be measured more by what the public don't know about a client than by what they do know. The legendary and comprehensively disgraced British practitioner Max Clifford, 'publicist to the stars', always claimed that 90% of his work involved keeping stories about his clientele out of the papers. (The bluffer should be aware that British PRs were always keen to emphasise that Max, as a self-proclaimed publicist, was definitely not one of their number.)

The journalist, trained to nail down and expose the truth, may well feel their instincts frustrated in a business where they will be expected to tailor the truth to present their client in the best possible light.

The other surprising thing is that it is an observed and proven fact that a journalist may spend decades receiving, reading and regurgitating press releases yet still not have the slightest clue how to write one.

Why, then, do so many of them make the move?

Because the pay is better, the relationships with business or political leaders, writers or performers, are naturally warmer when you are shielding them from awkward questions rather than asking them, and job security is infinitely greater. Indeed, as print circulations contract and the idea gains ground that you can get any idiot to write your web content for free, in the interests of self-promotion, there may soon be no real journalists left for all the ex-journalists working in PR to talk to.

Everyone employed in public relations is having so much fun that it could surely never be categorised as 'work' in the normal sense of the word.

EX-MILITARY TYPES

The British upper classes used to send their brighter younger sons into the church, and the dimmer ones into the armed forces. The former constituted a job for life, but the latter only did so in the event of a glorious death on the battlefield. Otherwise military discharge at a comparatively young age for middle-ranking officers left some years to fill before the inevitable encounter with the Grim Reaper. In the years after the Second World War PR came to seem a comfortable berth for many of these former soldiers, particularly those whose innumeracy presented a challenge in more traditional upper-crust callings like stockbroking.

Smooth, confident, calm in a crisis, and with a steady hand when pouring a pink gin, the ex-Army, Navy or RAF PR man was a very recognisable type now sadly fading from the scene as age wearies them and the years condemn.

GLUTTONS, CHAIN-SMOKERS AND DRUNKS

Back in the 1970s London boasted a reasonably famous pair of City PRs known to all simply as 'The Fat Boys', for entirely obvious reasons. They lived for lunch, and when they weren't lunching with journalists and/or clients they were in the pub.

In PR agencies with well-stocked drinks cabinets in every meeting room it was still possible to find executives who felt the need to secrete bottles of gin and whisky in their filing cabinets, and who would rub their hands with glee at the prospect of gaining a new client that would require 'a lot of knife and fork work'.

Lunches through into the 1990s would comprise an aperitif, ample quantities of wine (asking 'red or white?', even at a lunch for just two people, was considered positively puritanical by many) and digestifs of port, brandy or Kümmel. After which it would be considered impolite not to repair to the pub next door for a pint or three of beer just to settle the stomach.

Whether 'working' in the office or lunching, most PRs would have a cigarette on the go as well. Rooms that were not smoke-filled were regarded with suspicion.

Some lucky survivors of this era still work in PR to this day, sneaking out to old-fashioned restaurants to reminisce with their ever diminishing circle of contemporaries. Soon enough, like the last propagandists of the Second World War, they will all have staggered, belched and farted into history.

LECHERS

While consumer PR agencies were frequently run by powerful and capable women, the traditional late 20th century corporate or financial PR agency pitching team always comprised a grey-haired male managing director or partner, vastly experienced in the business, to convey a reassuring air of gravitas and to conduct the bulk of the pitch; a spotty but eager young male who would actually have written the presentation, and would do the bulk of the work were the pitch to prove successful; and a beautiful woman in a short skirt whose principal function was to look attractive.

To meet this requirement, PR consultancies of every type always seemed to employ a disproportionate number of beautiful women, and men who were attracted to beautiful women consequently found them more than averagely appealing places to work.

Nearly all of the beautiful women were driven by ambition: many to take the useless male MD's place on the board, some simply to find a rich husband. Naturally the latter hopes were focused on their plutocratic clientele rather than their usually drunken colleagues.

The lecher's life in PR therefore tended to be one of disappointment, except when sounder instincts fell victim to an excess of alcohol.

UNSACKABLES

The classic head of PR in a British business was a gentleman of a certain age who had failed in every more useful function, such as running a factory or adding up the numbers, but could not be fired for one reason or another. In some instances he was a scion of the founding family; in others he knew where various bodies were buried and therefore had the capacity to embarrass or otherwise damage members of the board. More frequently he was just a nice old boy whose long and faithful service was rewarded with a sinecure pending the maturity of his final salary pension. In this respect he resembled nothing so much as an old, incontinent dog that no one quite had the heart to take on its final journey to the vet.

Given that there is an actual job to be done in internal and external communications, even in the sleepiest organisation, the unsackable in-house PR's principal role in life was to recruit and retain an external PR consultancy capable of doing his job for him. In making his selection, the pulchritude of the inevitable beautiful woman on the pitching team often proved a decisive factor.

BORES

Being a bore has certainly never been a job requirement in PR, but it is a fact that large numbers of extremely boring people have found employment in the business. If you doubt this, go to a PR company's cocktail party and someone will unfailingly steer you towards the most boring man (it is always a man) you have ever met in your life. A man who can be guaranteed to turn your thoughts to murder or suicide within minutes, even if you have just celebrated the birth of your first child and a middling win on the National Lottery. One senior London PR executive was nicknamed Hundredweight

(CWT) after a stockbroker compared enduring lunch with him to Chinese Water Torture. Another was known as Titanium on the grounds that mining for the famously durable metal was easier than talking to him.

GRADUATES IN PUBLIC RELATIONS

Well within living memory, relatively small numbers of people were actually paid by the State to attend university courses in abstruse subjects like Latin or theology. Now the State expects a high proportion of school-leavers to run up huge lifetime debts in order to obtain degrees, and this naturally encourages them to favour 'practical' courses that will enhance their chances of obtaining a good job at the end of the course, and earning loads of wonga.

In the UK alone there are 83 different degree courses in public relations at the time of writing, some combining PR with reasonably logical adjuncts such as Journalism, Marketing and Advertising. Staffordshire University offers a memorably specialist course in Games Journalism and PR, but sadly the once fabled combined course in Public Relations and Dance no longer appears to be on offer anywhere. So removing the appealing possibility of a PR agency team that regularly began its pitches with a high-kicking routine in the style made famous by Busby Berkeley.

Just as by no means all theology graduates entered the church, we must assume that some with BA (Hons) in PR after their name go on to obtain useful jobs. But the majority must surely end up in the PR industry.

Even more than the demise of the drunken PR lunch,

this must surely be the greatest change to have occurred in the nearly three decades since the previous edition of *The Bluffer's Guide to Public Relations* was written. For that declared – quite rightly at the time – that the only essential qualification for PR, apart from being a bluffer, was to have undertaken some other job before attempting it.

PR skills, it was felt, were honed by long and bitter experience, and could not be taught any other way.

On exactly the same principle, it was once considered axiomatic that no one should embark upon a career in politics until they had obtained some experience of working in the real world, whether as a coal miner, manager, teacher, doctor or lawyer; it was also felt entirely right and proper that they should maintain those interests in parallel with service as a Member of Parliament, and the hours of House of Commons sittings were arranged to facilitate this.

Now politics, like PR, has become a career choice of its own, and any attempt to maintain interests outside it is portrayed as a gross dereliction of duty. The fact that this development has coincided with an observably massive increase in the incompetence of those in positions of political power is surely entirely coincidental.

There is at least one plus side to the growth of PR in academia. Since it is a truth universally acknowledged that those who can, do, while those who can't, teach, all those university courses must surely be taught by individuals who could not make a living doing actual PR. It is encouraging to know that there remains a cosy berth for the old unsackables who would once have kept their heads down as the in-house PR counsel, while protecting the sacrosanct tradition of the long lunch.

THE TWO PR OPTIONS

There are two main avenues for employment in public relations: working to improve understanding of an organisation that actually has some other useful purpose (in-house PR) or working for an organisation that exists solely to sell PR services (consultancy). It is entirely possible that the largest and most successful PR businesses will embrace the full gallimaufry of corporate job creation and employ an in-house PR to publicise their successes (or, more likely, minimise their failures) and encourage joyous bonding within the organisation, but frankly this line-blurring exceptionalism is too mind-blowing to be explored further.

THE ADVANTAGES OF BEING AN IN-HOUSE PR

- You only need to cater for the needs of one egomaniac client.
- If the organisation does something you actually approve of, such as trying to find a cure for cancer or dementia, you might even be able to convince yourself that you are doing something socially useful.

- You are likely to learn lots of corporate secrets that might create opportunities for industrial espionage or blackmail.
- Your stress levels are likely to be lower than in consultancy since you only have to service one client, who with any luck will be too busy and important to pay you much attention.
- Statistically, in-house roles in the UK private sector pay more on average than comparable work in consultancies.
- Depending on the size of the business, there may well be benefits such as a staff discount, company car and private health insurance.
- You might hope for progression up the career ladder all the way to board level.
- The company might even offer some sort of pension scheme.

If the organisation does something you actually approve of, such as trying to find a cure for cancer or dementia, you might even be able to convince yourself that you are doing something socially useful.

THE DISADVANTAGES OF BEING AN IN-HOUSE PR

- Since the egomaniac client is your sole source of income, you can't afford to tell them unwelcome truths.
- Willingness or refusal to sleep with the egomaniac

client are both ultimately likely to prove career-damaging.
- Horizons may narrow as you spend all your time focusing on the widget, cake, bar or interplanetary craft that the company produces or markets.
- If you do rise all the way to board level you will be left in little doubt that you are the least important member of said board.

THE ADVANTAGES OF WORKING IN A CONSULTANCY

- You will have a range of egomaniac clients, some of whom might even prove to be moderately interesting.
- Having a diverse income stream increases the chances of being able to offer helpfully frank advice.
- There will be more opportunities to build up a valuable favour bank with the media by disclosing awkward facts about the clients you don't like, or you believe are about to sack you.
- Opportunities for promotion and hence pay rises are likely to be greater than they would be working in-house.
- You are unlikely to live long enough to worry about a pension.

THE DISADVANTAGES OF WORKING IN A CONSULTANCY

- You have to spend your life pretending to the client you are talking to at the time that they are the only one that really matters.
- A disproportionate amount of your life will have to be

devoted to new business pitches, to offset your recurrent failure to achieve client satisfaction on the point above.

- Unavailability to existing clients owing to your devotion to new business pitches is likely to prompt them to consider moving their account, thereby precipitating another round of new business pitches. If you want to present this in a positive light, talk about it as an example of 'the circular economy'.
- Despite your theoretical independence, you are statistically unlikely to shake off the PR's inbuilt tendency always to try to tell clients what you think they want to hear.
- Your stress levels are likely to be stratospheric.
- You are unlikely to live long enough to worry about a pension.

So the choice is essentially one between a relatively easy life in which you will spend a lot of your time trying to second guess what your boss would like to hear; and a more varied but even more stressful one in which you will spend a lot of your time trying to second guess what a range of clients would like to hear. In making your choice, you may wish to reflect upon the fact that there are more depressed but diligent older people working in-house and more good-looking and wildly enthusiastic young people working in consultancies.

JOINING AN ESTABLISHED CONSULTANCY

Before seeking employment in a consultancy, you will naturally undertake extensive research to establish whether there is a good fit between its personality and your own. This will involve looking at selected agencies' websites for as long as you can bear it, and ranking them according to your ability to understand what the hell they are trying to say. Penalties are naturally imposed for the use of buzzwords that are irritating, clichéd and/or entirely meaningless. You will also review the pictures and biographies of senior team members to assess whether it might be bearable to advance your career prospects by embarking on a relationship with them, or may look forward to advancement through their death by natural causes such as cirrhosis, apoplexy or old age.

It is also worth Googling the agency's name along with the word 'scandal' to see if it has a track record of working for dodgy clients or a reputation as a front for the Mafia or Russian security service. Membership of a recognised PR trade body is usually considered to make it less likely that this will be the case.

When invited to an interview, remember to look massively eager and obliging, and to nod vigorously in agreement with comments from the interviewing panel even if you have not got the faintest clue what they are talking about. If you are just beginning your career in PR, also be prepared to accept a more lowly role in the organisation than the one for which you may feel qualified by your enormous talents. Promotion in PR consultancies can be exceedingly rapid if you prove your worth either by suggesting a brilliant idea that helps to win a new client, or simply by making a cracking cup of coffee.

TOP BLUFFING TIPS FOR INTERVIEW

Do say	*Don't say*
This is the only agency I have ever wanted to work for	*This is the only agency that would give me an interview*
I look upon you personally as a role model within the industry	*Sorry, what was your name again?*
In five years' time I'd like to be well on the way to doing your job	*In five years' time I'd hope to have finished the novel I'm writing*
In five years' time I'd hope to be earning enough to put down a deposit on a flat	*In five years' time I'd hope to have finished the novel I'm reading*
I like to think I would always adhere to the very highest ethical standards*	*Let's cut to the chase: take me on and I'll remind you what Monica did for Bill Clinton**

SETTING UP YOUR OWN CONSULTANCY

Clearly the ultimate way to secure freedom and riches in PR is to set up your own business, either with your own name over the door, or a jumble of letters (and perhaps, radically, numbers), or the name of some place/house/boat/writer/composer that means a great deal to you, and which you can talk about to promote an air of intellectual sophistication in future interviews.

This route will naturally appeal to those with

---

* Depending on your assessment of the character of the interviewer, and the nature of the agency, it may be advantageous to reverse the order of these suggestions: please exercise individual discretion. In the unlikely event of interviewer taking exception to apparently being offered a sexual favour, smile sweetly and say that you were obviously referring to the massive publicity generated by the liaison.

entrepreneurial instincts or, as it is also known, avarice. The snag with setting up your own PR business is that, unlike a widget manufacturer or most other sorts of service business, you are essentially the product and the guarantee of the organisation's future income stream. Hence there is no obvious lucrative exit route other than by selling your business to another consultancy or group with the promise that you will continue to work for them for some time.

There is also the conundrum that you probably went into PR in the first place because you enjoyed doing PR, but if you set up your own consultancy and it enjoys any success, you will spend less and less time doing PR and progressively more time managing the prima donnas that work for you. This can create confusion in the mind of the client, too, in both new and established PR businesses: is the person at the head of the consultancy there because they are a senior and credible adviser, or simply because they have the patience to supervise a bunch of flaky young people with a taste for talking nonsense, snorting cocaine and having personal relationship crises?

ß

A key part of the in-house PR's role is avoiding enquiries, whether from senior members of their own management about what they do all day, or from external nuisances such as customers, government bodies or the media. Particularly the media.

IN-HOUSE PR

AIMS AND PURPOSE

The prime aim of the in-house PR is to ensure the continued employment of the in-house PR. His or her first priority will therefore always be the recruitment of an external PR consultancy to provide operational support and, critically, to take the blame when things go wrong, as they almost certainly will.

Though of strictly secondary importance, the in-house PR will also be responsible for ensuring the protection of the corporate brand, the effective communication of its strategy and rare resulting successes, the maintenance of the organisation's website, and internal communications with his or her fellow employees.

INTERNAL COMMUNICATIONS

Let us suppose that a company wishes to increase its profitability, for the prime purpose of enlarging the directors' bonus pool, and decides that the best way to do this is by merging two factories into one, so making approximately

500 people redundant. Having taken this decision behind closed doors, the board will summon the in-house PR to draft two announcements: one to the shareholders making clear that this is the action of a board totally committed to maximising profitability in their interest; and another to the affected employees emphasising that the decision has been taken with the utmost regret, but also entirely in their own long-term interests.

Depending on the sector in which the company operates, further distinct announcements may also be required. For example, companies operating in the food manufacturing industry often attempt to tell wildly different stories to farmers, customers, shareholders, staff and the government.

In these situations, it is very important to use the right terminology:

Don't say	Do say
Human resources, personnel	People
Staff, employees	Colleagues
Decision	Consultation
Closure	Restructure
Fired	Examining all opportunities for redeployment
Sacked	Made voluntarily redundant as a last resort

Other and happier announcements will need to be drafted on matters such as the annual pay review, in which the PR will have to explain to their colleagues that hard times preclude all but the most modest inflation-linked increase, at the same time as the directors are awarding themselves a generous package of salaries, bonuses and LTIPs (Long Term Incentive Plans) 'to ensure that the company can retain the top talent it needs to prosper in an intensively competitive market, in the best interests of all its stakeholders'.

Then there are the regular messages to be written about the corporate dress code, striving to find a polite way of conveying the fact that fat people should avoid wearing leggings; about the use and abuse of the canteen, toilets and car park; and about the annual Christmas party, with special reference to drunkenness, the photocopying of genitalia, and the penalties for threatening or using violence against members of the management team.

When Churchill described Russian intentions in 1939 as 'a riddle, wrapped in a mystery, inside an enigma' he could well have been describing the epic inaccessibility achieved by many corporate PR departments.

AVOIDING ENQUIRIES

A key part of the in-house PR's role is avoiding enquiries, whether from senior members of their own management about what they do all day, or from external nuisances such as customers, government bodies or the media. Particularly the media.

When Churchill described Russian intentions in 1939 as 'a riddle, wrapped in a mystery, inside an enigma' he could well have been describing the epic inaccessibility achieved by many corporate PR departments. You will typically scan the corporate website without finding the slightest trace of their telephone number. The UK's largest mobile phone company famously has a PR department that cannot be rung up.

The in-house PR may thoughtfully provide an email address, though with scant chance that they will ever actually respond to it; or they will offer one of those clunkingly difficult 'contact us' forms in which to encapsulate your enquiry or summarise your grievance, which will then vanish into the ether leaving not a wrack behind, unless you have had the presence of mind to take a screenshot.

A week or so later you will almost certainly find yourself filling in another 'contact us' form enquiring whether you are ever going to receive a response to what you asked on the previous 'contact us' form. If the in-house PR is in playful mood they may actually respond to this one, asking you to repeat your original enquiry, which they will then ignore again.

As time passes, you will realise that your only hope of getting through to anyone at all is to readdress your question to the external PR agency that the in-house PR has appointed to do all their actual work.

Alternatively, try writing to or emailing the company's chief executive. Obviously they will never see your message themselves, but they will almost certainly have an efficient PA who will forward it to the in-house PR to deal with. Enquiries made by this route have a much higher chance of receiving a reply than those submitted direct.

CHOOSING AND LIAISING WITH EXTERNAL ADVISERS

For the in-house PR, selection of the right external agency to support – i.e. 'do all of' – his or her work is absolutely crucial. They must be intelligent and creative enough to generate a steady stream of bright ideas for which the in-house PR can take or at the very least share credit. But they must on no account be so utterly brilliant that they expose the in-house team as the bunch of lazy plodders they are almost certain to be.

The agency's offices should ideally be located a fair distance away from the in-house's corporate HQ, so that any meeting with them on the agency's own ground can be preceded and followed by a long and leisurely train journey. Ideally, this will permit a single brainstorming meeting to write off an entire working day. A suitable degree of physical remoteness will also reduce the risk of the agency making direct contact with the in-house PR's senior management team in ways liable to undermine his or her cosy sinecure.

Above all, though, the chosen agency must be one that is prepared to take it on the chin and accept 100% of the blame when PR initiatives fail to deliver the promised results, as they usually do.

THE CORPORATE NEWSPAPER

Any organisation of substance would once have aspired

to produce its own internal newspaper or magazine to share news about corporate achievements and the minutiae of its peoples' lives: a list of those who have endured 25 years in its employment; little vignettes about those members of staff who have appeared on TV talent shows or done wonderful things for charity; the introduction of an exciting new menu in the staff canteen; an explanation of why the air conditioning consistently fails to work during the hottest week of the year, but guarantees sub-zero temperatures when it is cold outside; but mainly, of course, features underlining what a truly wonderful, far-sighted and generous person the chief executive is, and what a privilege it is for all to have such a paragon as their leader.

Many companies, partnerships and charities still produce such a newspaper or e-newsletter, and the in-house PR will spend much time helping to pull it together, unless they have had the good sense or fortune to contract it out to a specialist publisher. Nowadays, though, the main avenues of communication within an organisation are the intranet or closed groups on social media. The in-house PR will craft warm introductory words about how the chief executive takes a keen personal interest in the views of all colleagues, and welcomes honest feedback. They will then spend much time deleting obscene and otherwise negative comments, and attempting to weed out from the group ex-employees bearing a grudge. Perhaps because redundancy has granted them more time on their hands, those who no longer work for an organisation always seem to be the most committed and colourful commentators about its numerous deficiencies.

CORPORATE SOCIAL RESPONSIBILITY (CSR)

The days are long gone when a company could justify its existence simply by making money; now it has to pretend that its real objective is doing good. The old school businessman might like to argue that providing jobs and paying tax on profits were actually doing a fair bit to help the community, but this sort of talk will cut little ice with Millennials and still less with Generation Z. To win favour with The Yoof, the organisation must develop a mission statement that emphasises its keen commitment to halting climate change, ending pollution, preventing cruelty, fighting inequality, eliminating all forms of discrimination, promoting diversity, curing disease and ultimately abolishing death. (Exceptions may be made in the last case for companies operating in specialist fields such as the manufacture of wreaths and coffins.)

All corporate initiatives must then conform with the agreed CSR agenda and be presented as a further sign of the organisation's pristine conscience and total commitment to doing the right thing at all times. If they seem to cynical outside observers likely also to increase sales or slash operating costs the in-house PR must wear a look of total surprise at the suggestion and murmur inscrutably 'that would be an entirely coincidental bonus'.

THE COMPANY CHARITABLE FOUNDATION

All self-respecting businesses will want to have their own charitable foundation, into which they can funnel the enthusiasm of their employees for raising money for good causes in their own time. This way, those funds can be channelled into the cause closest to the chief executive's own heart. One of the in-house PR's more testing roles will be explaining to the CEO that the law does not allow the charity to give direct support either to the business or to its senior management.

Typically, the organisation will choose a 'charity of the year' with which to ally itself. The in-house PR may expect to receive a steady stream of enquiries from his counterparts at external charities, asking how the 'charity of the year' is selected, and how best to put themselves forward for consideration.

The PR will usually explain that there is a 'one person, one vote' selection process, omitting to mention that the one person with a vote is the chief executive, and the chosen good cause is therefore overwhelmingly likely to reflect his or her own chosen leisure pursuits or family health preoccupations.

The PR will seek to encourage a focus on staff fundraising for the charitable foundation at times of year when business is slack or the workforce needs to be distracted from unpleasant realities such as the very long time that has elapsed since their last pay review. The PR will try to whip up enthusiasm for abseiling down the outside of head office, climbing Kilimanjaro, or cycling between every factory/store/office in the company by burbling on about the joys of teambuilding and working together to do something special for an exceptional cause.

The chief executive will then launch the lifeboat for which his colleagues' fundraising efforts have paid, and ensure that it is always on hand to shadow his new superyacht.

CONSUMER PR CONSULTANCY

AIMS AND PURPOSE

The overriding aim of the consumer PR consultancy is to persuade consumers to buy more of their clients' products. If the products are cakes, for example, the PR will seek to convince potential buyers, via the media, that their client's cakes are the most delicious cakes that anyone could ever imagine, even in their wildest and most drug-fuelled dreams. They will further seek to convey that these cakes are produced in unimpeachably hygienic conditions, by jolly, well-paid workers with a permanent song on their lips; that they contain no unnatural or unhealthy ingredients, and are only made with the finest organic flour, the purest cream and butter from ludicrously happy cows, and eggs laid by hens ranging freely across a National Park and scarcely able to believe their luck in being chosen to have their unborn chicks sacrificed for such a noble cause.

They will further emphasise that these cakes can be enjoyed without guilt not only about the sources of their ingredients and the manner of their production, but because they are bursting with health-giving properties, contain remarkably few calories and have amazingly low levels of fat, salt and sugar.

In short, the PR will seek to convince even the most ascetic, gluten-phobic misery that what they want above all else in life is a cake.

APPROACH

The first requirement of the consumer PR is to be relentlessly upbeat and perennially excited. Tiggerish levels of enthusiasm must be combined with a total refusal to take 'no' for an answer, or to admit the possibility of failure. Every mind-numbingly tedious message from the client – a slight change in the positioning of a glacé cherry, for example – must be hailed and then expounded as 'tremendously exciting news'.

Many hours will be spent in 'brainstorming' meetings to decide how best to describe the revolutionary glacé cherry breakthrough to the waiting world.

A junior member of the team will then be charged with preparing the first draft of a press release that will describe the new cake with the slightly repositioned glacé cherry with a level of excitement one might more readily associate with the news that Lord Lucan had just ridden into town on Shergar, explaining his long absence by the fact that he had been successfully developing a cure for motor neurone disease.

More senior members of the team will refine this draft through subtle amendments that appear, to the casual observer, to add little to its impact, but will be hailed by their 'super-excited' colleagues as *'totes amazeballs'* contributions that fall in no way short of total genius.

The first requirement of the consumer PR is to be relentlessly upbeat and perennially excited. Tiggerish levels of enthusiasm must be combined with a total refusal to take 'no' for an answer.

The PR will then send the final draft to the client, who will usually point out multiple factual errors and request a redraft. The process of exchanging redrafts with the client may continue for some time, until both parties are satisfied or one has lost the will to live. This will almost always be the one with less boundless optimism and enthusiasm, viz. the client.

'REACHING OUT'
Consumer PRs never send emails or make phone calls like normal people: they 'reach out', like a drowning

man on a sinking dinghy, and if they don't make contact the first time they will 'circle back' and 'reach out' again.

The 'reaching out' may extend to telephoning the hapless magazine employee or freelance in advance to whet their appetite for the 'tremendously exciting' press release that will be landing with them the next day. Then, shortly after they have emailed the breathlessly eager press release about the placement of the glacé cherry, they will ring again to 'make sure you have got it' and ask if there are any questions.

They will not be in the least discouraged if the answer is 'Well, I might well be reading the press release if I wasn't answering the bloody phone to you.'

Nor if, on the second follow-up phone call, the journalist suggests that it was, in fact, the most mind-numbingly tedious press release they had ever read, guaranteed to be of zero interest to their readers. They will just carry on trying to persuade the journalist that he or she is wrong.

In short, to succeed in consumer PR you should combine the intellect of a hamster, and the energy and enthusiasm of a springer spaniel, with the hide of a rhinoceros that has lived an unusually long and dangerous life.

Key phrases for success in consumer PR:

Do say	Don't say
This is an amazing opportunity	I know it's boring, but I've got a mortgage to pay
We're reaching out to masses of people	We've sent a group email

We've targeted all the key influencers	We've sent a group email
Can we jump on a call?	Please stop putting the phone down on me, or I will cry
There's a huge amount of interest	The number of people who have directly told me to f*** off is barely into double figures
The whole team has worked incredibly hard to secure this fantastic coverage	A really fatigued journalist with a space to fill actually cut and pasted the release

PHOTOGRAPHY

A picture is famously worth a thousand words. So the press release about the new cake with the slightly repositioned glacé cherry will naturally have to be accompanied by a truly awesome photograph of the product: one calculated to make the mouths of recipients water with keen anticipation.

This normally represents a massive challenge, addressed through the employment of specialist food stylists, set dressers, lighting technicians and camera operators to create an image that does indeed look rather delicious, though sadly bears little resemblance to the product that will be on sale to the public at large.

SAMPLING

Whatever its product, one can be sure that the client will have supreme confidence in it, and will feel that the best way to convince the media of its many superior qualities is to allow them to try it. It then falls to the

PR either (a) to think of some convincing reasons why this is likely to prove counterproductive, or (b) to make arrangements for getting said product into the hands of those most likely to write positive things about it.

In the case of a food product – say, a cake – this might seem deceptively simple. But what sort of cake is it? Ambient, chilled or frozen? ('Ambient' is how the food industry describes stuff that can be stored, moved around and sold at normal room temperatures rather than in a chiller or freezer.)

Even getting an ambient cake into the hands of a journalist presents a range of logistical challenges, from the legendary incompetence and unreliability of almost all courier companies to the equally renowned jobsworth unhelpfulness of those manning most media reception desks. ('What if I sign for this and it turns out to be poison – or a bomb?')

These difficulties are substantially increased if the product needs to be maintained in a temperature-controlled environment. Long experience of attempting to place frozen food in the hands of journalists before it becomes the centrepiece of a puddle suggests that it is almost unachievable. Unless, of course, one can bring the journalist to the frozen food.

ORGANISING EVENTS

This brings us to the next key item on the consumer PR's 'to do' list: organising events to show off the client's products, stores or services to the potential puff-writing community (which these days may well comprise more bloggers, vloggers and social media stars than actual old-fashioned journalists).

For a client in the food or fashion industries, regular events must be held to showcase the next season's 'must have' lines. For food companies, this means showing off barbecue lines in January and, famously, holding 'Christmas in July'. Though that month has now become so crowded that many are seeking to get ahead of the pack by holding 'Christmas in July' in June.

The original logic for this apparent madness was the overwhelming importance of securing favourable coverage in glossy magazines that have long production lead times. As sales of printed media dwindle and reliance on the internet increases, this becomes of less importance and creates the risk that early saturation coverage of the forthcoming delights of Christmas will mean that they create zero excitement when the selling season actually arrives.

For the consumer PR, there are few joys to compare with serving roast turkey and all the trimmings to a large gathering of hacks on what is almost guaranteed to be the hottest day of the summer in the northern hemisphere.

Similarly, all press fashion shows have to be held approximately six months ahead of the products actually arriving in stores. The age-old rules of retailing also demand that the clothing and footwear will reach the stores at least a couple of months before there is any demand for them, to guarantee that there will be no swimwear on sale when the sun is actually shining, and no thick coats available during a blizzard, because by then the store will only be stocking its exciting new spring range.

STUNTS

Clients love a publicity stunt, particularly if it actually generates some publicity. It encourages them to believe that they are dealing with creative geniuses rather than mere tradespeople, working their way through the standard motions of writing and issuing a press release. In consequence, the CEO may well be persuaded to take part in person, being filmed as they make their stunt arrival via drone, hot air balloon or zipwire, even though the likeliest outcome is an appearance on *Have I Got News For You* focusing on their pained expression, with a lipreader deciphering their inaudible words as 'Jesus Christ, me poor bollocks'.

Outcome of stunt:	PR must say:
Positive coverage	It was a fantastic idea, brilliantly executed
Embarrassing coverage	There is no such thing as bad publicity
No coverage	We always said that it was a high-risk venture
Negative coverage	Remember it's tomorrow's chip wrapper

DEMONSTRATING ROI

In order to justify a continuing (and ideally increasing) fat fee, the consumer PR consultancy will have to spend a great deal of time compiling reports to demonstrate what an awesome job it is doing, and to prove that it is delivering a great ROI. (Not a French monarch with a fetish for capitalisation, but Return On Investment.)

If the consultancy charges for its time by the hour (as almost all do), the more time it spends compiling reports to prove its own brilliance, the greater the fee it will be able to justify. This is the PR equivalent of the secret of perpetual motion.

Traditionally, PRs attempted to measure their added value by totting up the column inches they claimed to have generated each week or month, and then telling the client how much it would have cost them to buy the same amount of advertising space. This was known as AVE or Advertising Value Equivalence.

This approach always made PR look brilliant value, particularly since Mr and Mrs Average are more likely to read and believe something presented as editorial rather than a paid ad, however brilliant, which they are highly liable to skim over and/or discount.

However, AVE is now acknowledged by all right thinkers to be total nonsense, leading us into a Brave New World encapsulated in every PR's favourite leisure reading, the Barcelona Principles of 2010 – so called, unsurprisingly, because they were agreed at a conference held in that Spanish (or, if you prefer, Catalan) city under the auspices of the snappily titled International Association for Measurement and Evaluation of Communication. Representatives of PR firms from 33 countries attended, and the eyes of Barcelona bar owners still grow misty at the memory.

The Barcelona Principles:

What they say	What they mean
Goal setting and measurement are important	Have a vague idea of what you're trying to do before you start, then see how it works out
Measure outcomes rather than outputs	Has the client sold more stuff than it would have done without your efforts, or otherwise become better regarded?
Measure the impact on business results	Is the client better off?
Measure media results by quality as well as quantity	Take account of tone, credibility and message delivery as well as simple column inches
AVEs are not the value of PR	AVE is a load of crap, man
Social media can and should be measured	Though we've yet to work out exactly how
Measurement must be transparent and replicable	Don't fiddle the figures to justify a higher fee

The bottom line of all this is that PRs can no longer say 'look at all those column inches – it would have cost you millions to buy that space!' They must instead drone on endlessly about media impressions, message pull-through, opportunities to view, reach, tweets, likes and click-throughs. (Google 'measuring ROI of public relations' for a brief introduction to an all but incomprehensible dystopia, where assorted snake oil salesmen will seek to convince you that they have indeed discovered a patented way to measure the immeasurable.)

Do say	Don't say
We totally believe in the Barcelona Principles	I always thought Real Madrid was a better team

For a consumer PR company, the simple answer might seem to be to try to correlate PR activity with sales. 'We ran a PR campaign for the cake with the repositioned glacé cherry, and sales of it doubled.'

Ah, but *post hoc* is not necessarily *propter hoc*. Maybe the entirely coincidental (and wholly inaccurate) report that glacé cherries have a Viagra-like impact on the sexual potency and appetite of the over-50s also played a part, and sales would have soared without any PR input at all.

At this point, the canny PR bluffer will suggest:

COMMISSIONING RESEARCH

Market research is a brilliant way of justifying to the client what you were planning to do anyway, and proving that your PR work is adding massive value. Correct framing of the questions and selection of the right sample should ensure that independent market research will prove almost anything you want. Even better than that, you can justify repeating the exercise regularly to monitor the steady improvement in perceptions of the client that you are being paid to deliver. And, in what may seem to many like the perfect crime, you can pocket a fat commission from every survey you organise!

FEES, EXPENSES AND MARK-UPS

The client engaging a PR agency normally negotiates an annual fee, and naively assumes that this will cover all PR activities for the coming year. They could not be more wrong.

For a start, the agency will base its fee on a calculation of how much of its time the client will take up, among staff at varying levels of seniority. They will then spend a chunk of the hours the client has paid for laboriously compiling time sheets so that they can compare actual and budgeted time employed, and justify lobbying for an early fee increase.

In addition, the agency will expect to make additional charges for just about everything it does. In the olden days, much friction used to arise when the client received its first monthly bill and discovered that the fee it was paying did not cover such basics as making telephone calls, printing, photocopying, postage, or providing tea and biscuits.

While it is hard to justify imposing an additional charge each time the PR presses 'send' on an email, there is still a plethora of additional billing opportunities including but by no means restricted to media monitoring, travel (always first class by rail, and business class by air), accommodation, entertaining and the aforementioned market research. Even better than that, by an ancient tradition adopted from the advertising industry, PR consultancies traditionally 'mark up' such expenses by 17.65%, to compensate themselves for the trouble of making out the bill.

One client is known to have demanded a justification for the arbitrary addition of 17.65% to its expenses bills. After due consideration, the agency responded by increasing its mark-up to 30.0%.

CORPORATE PR CONSULTANCY

AIMS AND PURPOSE

The objective of corporate PR is to enhance the reputation of a company in general, and almost invariably of its egomaniac leader in particular. Because, clearly, Hann's Widgets would ultimately sell more widgets and make more money for its owner Mr Hann if customers, suppliers, employees, unions, regulators, commentators, landlords, quangos, trade associations and the public at large had a better understanding of the company's strategy, values and cutting-edge commitment to equality of opportunity, diversity, sustainability and philanthropy.

As part of this process, Mr Hann might well become conveniently identified as the nation's 'go to' expert on widgets, so that he is rarely off the TV and radio news, and is a regular guest on discussion programmes and panel shows. So that, as well as being a titan of industry, he also becomes something of a celebrity – something he never wanted, but will bear manfully in the interests of all the other stakeholders in his business. Just as, when a touch of the monarch's sword elevates him from plain Mr to Sir Optimus Hann, he will claim with a straight face that he never dreamt of such an honour, and has accepted it only on behalf of the Widgets team as a whole, and in order to give Mrs Hann her long-overdue official recognition as a Lady. Obviously, as a good bluffer, you will instantly recognise this as the self-serving twaddle it undoubtedly is, and wear a suitably wry smile when conveying it to the media.

Much time can be profitably wasted analysing the competition, and establishing how and why they are better regarded than the client.

DEFINING OBJECTIVES

Any incoming consultancy will have made much in its pitch of the importance of 'defining objectives': establishing where the business is at (hopefully an industry also-ran offering much scope for easy improvement) and where it would like to be in, say, five years' time. (In practice it is always five years' time, for some reason: never three, seven or ten.)

Much time can then be profitably wasted analysing the competition, and establishing how and why they are better regarded than the client. Key target audiences need to be identified and analysed, corporate values agreed, messages defined, spokespeople chosen and trained, and a multi-year, multi-channel communications campaign developed, refined and accepted before any actual communicating can begin.

SEEKING UNIQUENESS

Corporately speaking, what sets Hann's Widgets apart? Technology? Investment? Cost-effectiveness of production? The amazing diversity of its workforce? The fact that a percentage of the profit from every widget sold is used to fund an orphanage in Africa, a medical research laboratory in Cambridge, or an institute dedicated to the promotion of global peace? Or simply the fact that it is led by an individual of towering genius?

DEVELOPING CORPORATE IDENTITY AND BRANDING

In an industry filled with bluffers, the supreme exponents of the craft are surely those who manage to convince business leaders who have not been sectioned under the Mental Health Act that it will add to the value of their company if they change its name from something dull and descriptive (like Hann's Widgets) to one that is memorable, meaningless and non-restrictive.

Traditionally forged by a roomful of men in well-worn jeans with strokeable beards and pony-tails, but these days probably randomly generated by computers, there is a list from Accenture to Zeneca of new corporate names that have been conjured up in an attempt either to bury unfortunate past associations or simply create an image of an organisation that is exciting, modern and generally 'down with the kids'.

Once upon a time companies simply condensed their names into initials, like the once-famous conglomerate BTR (now, inevitably, renamed Invensys). But know-alls would always add (formerly British Tyre & Rubber) in brackets, and initials can often turn out also to stand for other things, often with unpleasant associations. Besides, it could be proven that some of the best-known corporate brands of all time were totally meaningless: notably Kodak, which was plucked from thin air by George Eastman because he judged, correctly, that it would be a more memorable name than his own.

And so the venerable Norwich Union became Aviva. Not to be confused with Arriva, which used to be a Sunderland-based motor dealer called T. Cowie. Or Aveda, which is an American hair products business. Or Aveva, which is an information technology company based in Cambridge, England. The cynic might note that the search for uniquely memorable names seems to lead to ones that are quite easily confused with each other.

Amazingly, there are very few instances in which totally meaningless new corporate names have been abandoned in the face of public and media mockery. The reversion of Consignia to Royal Mail in the UK is without doubt the best-known example.

Choosing the new name is just the start, of course. The newly named company will also require a dynamic new logo, and design standards will have to be set out dictating exactly how this should appear on signage, vehicles, letterheads, business cards etc.

None of this highly specialised work is actually the responsibility of the corporate communications consultancy. But they will most probably set the ball rolling by suggesting to the client how much easier achieving their clearly defined objectives would be if only the company had an exciting new name; will happen to know just the right experts to do the work; will lead the applause when it is unveiled; and disseminate massively excited press releases designed to ensure that the response to the new branding is characterised by euphoria at best, and understanding at worst, and never by indifference or ridicule.

They will also, it may be assumed, pocket a fat commission from the corporate branding consultancy in return for the introduction.

THE PROFILE OPPORTUNITY

We are, for the most part, human beings. We like to read about other human beings, if we can't read about cute animals or scary zombies. Hence it is remarkably difficult to place media stories about a corporation, but relatively easy to do so if the focus is on the company's leader. Particularly if said leader has actually done something interesting, or is liable to make comments that are eye-catchingly controversial.

The bluffer will naturally set the client's expectations suitably low. While the pitch document might have promised 'a full page press profile of the CEO' it will be swiftly explained after appointment that securing this in a national daily or Sunday title falls very much towards the end of the five-year plan. Much better, in the short term, to focus on the local newspaper that is surviving by the skin of its teeth and will print pretty much anything. (With any luck, it will turn out that the CEO and all his family and friends are avid readers of the *Penistone Examiner* and rarely look at the *Financial Times*.)

Then there are trade publications covering every imaginable sector (most, amazingly, boast rival titles), which should be a pushover when the PR suggests that they might like to write about the client.

And, if all else fails, there is a plethora of vanity publications that will write about any chief executive – and even allow you to adjust the copy before publication so that the client appears to say what they were meant to say, rather than what they actually came out with.

What the corporate PR thinks	What the corporate PR says
Oh Jesus	I think what Sir Optimus meant to say was …
I haven't got a blanking clue	I'll have to get back to you on that

BLUFFER'S TIP: *Any publication that offers copy approval and/or asserts that appearing in it will be 'at no cost to you' is completely worthless and will be read by absolutely no one. It will also be 'at no cost to you' because they will take the opportunity to pester every supplier and other business tenuously connected with your client to buy advertising space to accompany the feature. However, so long as you don't tell the client any of this they may still be delighted* *by their appearance in* World-Beating CEOs Magazine *and enjoy looking at a framed copy of the article in their office.*

It is often the case that the CEO will have a challenging personality, destined to be memorialised as one 'who did not suffer fools gladly'. This is the obituarist's standard formula for 'was a total bastard'. If this is the case, the following checklist of excuses may come in handy:

What it looks like	What to call it
Unbelievable rudeness	Shyness
Arrogance	A surprising lack of self-confidence
Impatience	Enthusiasm
Being catatonically boring	Impressive mastery of detail
Ignorance of basic facts	Temporary amnesia

FAME AT LAST

When the client finally achieves sufficient eminence to be interviewed for a profile in a national news title, it is important to bear in mind that these almost always follow a formula that includes snippets of information (e.g. favourite book and film) or invite the subject to choose between two alternatives (e.g. full English or muesli? Parachute Regiment or Waffen SS?) It is important that the client is fully briefed beforehand so that they do not give exactly the same answers as every previous interviewee (with special reference to Steve Jobs' autobiography and *The Shawshank Redemption*). It may also be useful to remind the client beforehand of their spouse's name and how many children they have.

PUBLIC SPEAKING

In order to build awareness of Hann's Widgets through its CEO, the PR will seek to exploit any and every opportunity for him or her to express their views on industry and more general issues. Bearing in mind that, if the CEO is a member of the BNP whose principal hobby is collecting Nazi memorabilia, very extensive rehearsal will be required before letting them loose in any forum where there is an opportunity for questions to be asked and a risk of them being answered honestly.

Industry conferences are a good place to start. Even if the client is mind-numbingly boring, they will be in good company; and if, by some miracle, they aren't, the conference will provide an ideally sheltered environment in which they can develop their public speaking skills with a view to their wider application.

Ghosting speeches. It is a very brave PR indeed who assumes that the client can be trusted to write and deliver his or her own speech on any occasion. The chair of the consultancy will promise to write it on the client's behalf, but will then delegate the task to another director, who will pass it on to an executive, who will hand it to a PA until – like every task in the agency – it ends up in the hands of the boy who is paid to weigh the parcels in the post room. If the boy does a half decent job, his career development will be stellar. If he doesn't there will be an entertaining bout of recriminations at every level in the agency, following which the task will be delegated to an external specialist. The chair of the consultancy will make one or two minor tweaks to this before presenting the finished product to the client, and claim credit for the entire work.

Promoting expertise. Try to identify an area other than Nazi memorabilia in which the client is actually an expert; one on which they can talk knowledgeably and confidently; and ideally one in which the media and public have some passing interest. Obesity, say, or climate change. Working out the relevance of a widget manufacturer to either of these may prove something of a challenge, but it is precisely this sort of creativity that justifies the corporate PR's very substantial fee.

Whenever any news story breaks within the chosen field of expertise, the corporate PR team will then email and ring around every broadcast organisation to ask whether they would like to have the benefit of the client's unique perspective on this development. There is a reasonable chance that at least one will be desperate enough to say yes.

REHEARSAL AND TRAINING

Before the client makes any appearance before an audience or a camera, it is important for the PR to ensure that they are rigorously rehearsed on the correct answer (or, more likely, evasion) to every question they are liable to be asked. Plus a long list more that they are never likely to be asked in practice, but which it is good training or simply high-quality entertainment to ask anyway. 'How dare you speak about family values when you have been conducting an affair with your PA for years?' is a good trial shot here.

BLUFFER'S TIP: *Many people make a good living out of something called 'media training', but you can do it yourself with these six simple tips:*

1. *Turn your mobile phone off before you start, or hand it to your PR.*
2. *Always look directly at the interviewer, not at the camera.*
3. *Don't let your gaze wander: you will look shifty if you do.*
4. *Don't wave your hands around: you will look barmy if you do.*
5. *Tell the interviewer what you want to say, not what they want to hear.*
6. *If you don't know the answer to the question, ask yourself another one and give the answer to that instead.*

THE SOFA, THE PANEL AND THE DESERT ISLAND

In the UK, the client may well feel a strong desire to take a seat on the sofa on breakfast TV or the BBC's *The One Show*, or to take part in a late night chat programme, or to participate in *Any Questions* or *Question Time*. Perhaps even to be a guest on *Desert Island Discs*. The role of the corporate PR is to badger the unfortunate producers of these programmes on what a great idea this would be; or, in the unlikely event of one of them making an approach to sound out the possibility of the client's involvement, to claim full credit for the 'amazing opportunity' that has fallen into the PR's lap.

If despatching a client to *Any Questions* or *Question Time*, it is important to brief them beforehand on which is still hosted by a Dimbleby, and to get them to understand the much higher degree of moronic audience participation in the TV version of the show, and the consequent need to keep any tendency towards intellectual arrogance firmly in check.

Choosing a play list for *Desert Island Discs* should never be left to the client in case they choose seven excerpts from Wagner operas, with the *Horst-Wessel-Lied* chucked in for light relief. The PR will be guided by the knowledge that too much opera or classical music will make the client seem like a snob, while professing an unlikely enthusiasm for grime or hip-hop will make the client sound like a phony, unless they are carefully introduced as being 'to remind me of my kids' (pause to wipe away a tear). For similar reasons, choice of the obligatory book and luxury item should never be left to the client.

THE REALITY DOCUMENTARY

Every well-known business in the UK has either featured in a 'reality' TV documentary series, or has turned down multiple approaches to participate in one. Whatever the TV production company may claim in its pitch, the reality is that all such series start with the self-same objective of maximising viewer numbers and will seek to do so by:

1. Making the client a laughing stock. If the client enjoys a joke this may turn out all right, though few captains of industry are noted either for self-deprecation or a sense of humour.
2. Conveying a perpetual sense of crisis. The key to viewer retention is 'jeopardy', and so every few minutes they will have to be nudged to stay tuned in by asking them to consider such questions as whether:
   - the new design of widget will work
   - the aspiring graduate trainee will pass their interview
   - the new 'gender neutral' lavatories will prove popular
   - the CEO's spouse will find out about his or her unusual hobby
   - the corporate PR that recommended participation in this farrago has still got a job.

Because it is correctly assumed that the average TV viewer now has the attention span of a gnat that has inhaled large quantities of hallucinogenic substances, all such programmes are constructed according to the old tripartite school essay format:

1. Tell them what you are going to say
2. Say it
3. Remind them of what you have said.

Since the undoubted highlight of the show for its producer and viewers alike will undoubtedly be the moment of maximum embarrassment for the client, this means that the cringe-making footage will be shown at least three times in the course of the broadcast; and, if it is aired on a commercial TV channel, is likely to be further repeated before and after every commercial break.

In the circumstances, it is important for the PR to make a careful evaluation of the size of the client's ego before responding to the production company's approach:

CEO personality and correct PR response to reality documentary approach:

1. **Total egomaniac.** Sure, when can you start filming?
2. **Average egomaniac.** We will need to make a careful evaluation of the likely impact of your proposal on the business before sending our regrets.
3. **Normal, easygoing person.** Sure, when can you start filming? (Because they are clearly in the wrong job and their inevitable sacking will provide 'jeopardy' of gold dust quality.)

In the all too likely case of unforeseen events halting or reversing progress on to the broad sunlit uplands of corporate prosperity … the role of the consultant is to portray this entirely temporary hiccough in the best possible light.

FINANCIAL PR CONSULTANCY

AIMS AND PURPOSE

The prime aims of the financial PR consultant are to inflate the already over-sized ego of the client's chief executive, and to ensure that investors, consumers, suppliers, competitors, landlords, politicians and civil servants (in the UK, particularly those involved in the compilation of the twice-yearly royal honours lists) are fully aware of the brilliance of the company's strategy, the matchless quality of its products and the unparalleled excellence of its financial performance and prospects.

These days, it is also important to explain that the company's success is not in any way related to the destruction of the rainforests or the impoverishment of communities anywhere in the world, but is driven by sound ethical principles of Sustainability (otherwise known as Corporate Social Responsibility, q.v.).

The company will also want to demonstrate its strong commitment to diversity and the financial PR will assist by assembling lots of baffling statistics that show massive opportunities within the organisation for all regardless of ethnicity, religion, age or disability, despite its being run by an almost entirely white, male and middle-aged board of directors.

In the all too likely case of unforeseen events halting or reversing progress on to the broad sunlit uplands of corporate prosperity, or resulting in a catastrophic environmental disaster, the role of the consultant is to portray this entirely temporary hiccough in the best possible light.

FINANCIAL CALENDAR REPORTING

This is the bread and butter of financial PR: announcing the company's quarterly, half-yearly and annual results and portraying them as positively as may be possible. The brief is always to achieve maximum coverage if the results are good, and to minimise it if they are not. Self-important financial PRs who wish to be recognised as strategic thought leaders will always insist that the company writes its own reports and press releases, or if – as is often the case – no one on the corporate payroll can actually write intelligible English, delegate the task to an out-of-work and grateful hack. The PR can then claim credit for inserting one or two critical pieces of spin that transform the draft from a disaster waiting to happen into a guaranteed triumph.

It is important to emphasise that there are no

circumstances whatsoever in which the chairman of the client company should be allowed to write the important page headlined 'Chairman's Statement'.

If all else fails and the PR can no find no alternative to writing the release or report himself, interest can be kept alive by the setting of small personal challenges. One year a financial PR company MD took pride in making 'This has been a watershed year for your company' the opening words of as many plc chairmen's statements as possible, and sitting back to see whether anyone noticed. No one did.

The invention of the word processor revolutionised the production of annual reports and press releases, as it did so many aspects of the PR's life. Now all he or she has to do is take last year's draft and change the odd word here and there to demonstrate consistency of strategic purpose, and fulfil the client's perennial desire to make it 'the same ... but different'. Do remember to insert the appropriate adjective, though: one UK food manufacturer's annual report memorably included the incontrovertible but unhelpful assertion that its cake-making subsidiary had 'had another year'.

It is always useful to retain drafts of releases and annual reports, particularly of the first one. At meetings the day before important announcements, as Draft 28a is being earnestly debated by the client and its multifarious advisers, it is customary for the client's chairman to suggest a brilliant improvement to the wording which will almost invariably turn out to mean reverting to exactly what the PR recommended in Draft 1. The role of the PR in these circumstances is to repress the desire to say 'I told you so' and assure the chairman that he is a towering genius.

Do say	Don't say
Perfect!	I told you so
Absolute genius!	Back to Draft 1, then. Great.

PRESS RELEASES

As with non-financial releases, the basic principles are simple: put the good news in the headline, if there is any, e.g. 'Hann's Widgets announces record sales and profits, and creates 2,000 new jobs'. If there is no good news, head it 'Trading update' and hope that no one will read it. Make up and include a stirring quote from the chief executive with the aim of ensuring that no one actually feels the need to ring him/her up and find out what he/she really feels about anything.

A key role of the Financial PR is to ensure that the client is never surprised, except by the massive size of the bill for the PR's services.

REHEARSALS

A key role of the PR is to ensure that the client is never surprised, except by the massive size of the bill for the PR's services. Hence all interactions with the media, analysts and investors must be exhaustively rehearsed, with the PR taking advantage of his or her inside knowledge to pose a series of questions that stand almost no chance of ever being asked in real life. But think of how grateful the client will be if the first question from Bill Spokes of the *Sun* the next day is 'How exactly would you cope if an asteroid struck your widget-making factory on Teesside at the same time as an outbreak of amoebic dysentery decimated your workforce in Brunei Darussalam?' And think of the pleasure that is always to be derived from being paid to make other people squirm.

PRESS CONFERENCES

A dying event now that the ranks of financial journalists have been so thinned, and constant online deadlines become so demanding. You will need a really exceptional story to justify holding a physical press conference rather than an online conference call. Even then, be sure to lower the client's expectations by speculating from the outset that no one will turn up. After which you should bribe a couple of out-of-work old mates to pitch up claiming to write for obscure trade publications. Tip them an extra tenner to mumble the details so that the client cannot check their credentials.

TIMING

The busiest days for routine financial releases are Tuesday to Thursday, because Monday creates the risk that you might actually have to work over the preceding weekend, and clients always suspect that people read the papers less attentively on a Saturday, and might therefore miss reports of their brilliance issued on a Friday. If you are prepared to bite the bullet of weekend working, Monday therefore represents a good opportunity to send out a release when there will be less competition around – with the caveat that it is also the traditional day for announcing major contested takeovers that are liable to drown out everything else.

PRs have devoted years to working out the best days to bury bad news. Thursday is traditionally the busiest day for financial news and not a bad bet, unless you are able to react opportunistically to an unexpected royal death, cabinet resignation, air crash or natural disaster. Hoary old wheezes like 'trying to slip it out' in the late afternoon before a bank holiday weekend, or around lunchtime on Christmas Eve, have a habit of backfiring spectacularly.

In the good old days the best way to soften the blow of bad financial news was considered to be leaking a mildly exaggerated version of the forthcoming Stock Exchange announcement to a favoured Sunday newspaper. Similarly, good news would be previewed by feeding the chosen paper a story that slightly understated the numbers to be reported. This allowed the actual announcement to be greeted with relief or elation that would, with any luck, be reflected in the price of the client's shares in the following morning's market reports. This practice, known as the 'Friday night drop' is severely frowned upon by government-appointed 21st century financial regulators, although it seems to remain a key feature of the government's own approach to communications.

THE ANNUAL GENERAL MEETING

The one day in the year on which the clients' directors actually have to meet their shareholders, and obtain their support for re-elections, and salary and bonus packages. Any British PR will naturally advise the client to hold this in a provincial hotel inconveniently distant from a railway station, and timed to begin before anyone catching the first fast train from London could hope to arrive. They will also advise strongly against the provision of inducements to attend, such as a free lunch or goodie bags stuffed with the company's products. One London brewer whose AGM was the occasion of a legendary free booze-up found its share register excessively complicated by the number of people who bought only one share to provide an entry ticket.

The PR will naturally rehearse the board on every possible difficult question that might be asked by a shareholder, in the unlikely event that anyone apart from particularly bored company pensioners actually bothers to turn up. Most of their enquiries are innocuous; indeed, one amusing ploy is for a questioner to read solemnly through every line of the annual profit and loss account from turnover to dividends, by way of gross profit, operating profit, pre-tax profit and earnings per share, thereby reducing the finance director to a gibbering wreck; and then conclude with 'so I would just like to congratulate the board on another excellent performance'.

Very occasionally a really tough wide ball shareholder question will slip through the PR's net. Luckily expert help will almost certainly be to hand among the huge array of talent on the board. At one AGM the lightly perspiring chairman was seen to receive a quickly handwritten note, passed along the board table from the highly experienced non-executive director at its far end. The invaluable advice it contained, which should cover most such eventualities, was 'Tell him to f*** off.'

EXECUTIVE REMUNERATION

One reason for delegating the tedious business of annual report writing is that no one actually reads the things, apart from interns and graduate trainees at major investing institutions, and obsessives at assorted lobbying groups. The one bit to which everyone turns, and at which a read report will inevitably fall open (like the juicy bit in *Lady Chatterley's Lover*) is the Directors' Remuneration Report revealing how much the company's leadership has pocketed during the last financial year.

There is no scope for self-justifying commentary within this report, so the PR must be prepared with a long list of justifications for this eye-watering largesse, usually pointing out how modest it is compared with the massive value that the brilliant management team has created for shareholders, and indeed with the outrageous rewards taken by the company's less successful peers.

The PR should never underestimate how literal-minded chief executives may be. Decades ago one of the first CEOs to breach the £1m salary barrier was advised by his financial PR firm that it might be politic to reward himself a little more modestly. The next year's report recorded his pay as £999,999.

EXECUTIVE DEPARTURES

The life of the CEO is rarely nasty, but often brutish and short. The competent financial PR will have a handy range of ready-made explanations for the abrupt departure of the client's leader:

Words	Meaning
'asked to resign by the board'	about to go to prison
'left by mutual agreement'	found with a hand in the till and/or paying sex workers/ drug dealers from corporate funds
'wishes to spend more time with his family'	fired for gross incompetence
'feels that the time is right to seek a new challenge'	fired for gross incompetence
'has decided to retire'	can't stand any more arguments about gross incompetence
'promoted to deputy chairman'	moved into the bed next to the door and given a meaningless title pending dismissal
'plans to go plural'	have made their pile and crave an easier life as a serial non-executive director

PHOTOSHOOTS

Never, ever underestimate the vanity and stupidity of your client, and their resulting willingness to do anything a photographer may ask of them. For this reason it is essential that all corporate photo opportunities are rigorously policed by the PR at all times. Otherwise you are likely to find yourself explaining to the CEO of your fashion retailing client that it is really not a great idea to be photographed manhandling apparently teenage models; or trying to bribe picture desks to delete the picture of your food company CEO cramming a whole giant pasty into his mouth, with which they like to illustrate their annual report of his remuneration package under a witty and original headline containing the words 'fat cat'.

Remember also to undertake a careful check of the background for any photographic shoot, looking particularly for any letters or words that might be abbreviated or otherwise wrenched out of context to show the client in an unfavourable light. If you hope to use the image more than once, also ensure that the client is not wearing a seasonal marker such as a Remembrance Day poppy or Christmas jumper.

INITIAL PUBLIC OFFERINGS (IPOS)

This is an opportunity for the public to buy shares in a company, and the role of the financial PR is to persuade investors that it is a once-in-a-lifetime opportunity to obtain shares in a business with fantastic prospects, at a bargain price. The PR must at all costs try to avoid anyone asking why, if this is the case, the existing owners are so keen to sell. Pitching for IPOs is an important part of the work of financial PRs because, unless they screw up the launch spectacularly, it usually marks the beginning of a long and reasonably lucrative relationship handling the company's financial calendar reporting. Or, as one comfortably retired financial PR CEO memorably describes it, 'money for old rope'.

MORE STUNTS

Even the grander and more rarefied field of financial PR is not immune to the client's belief that column inches are best generated through publicity stunts. In the glory days of UK privatisations, it was deemed impossible to announce the price of an IPO (q.v.) without members of the SAS abseiling down the face of a landmark building to unveil it, or equally luckless members of HM forces being assembled to spell it out on the deck of an aircraft carrier.

In brainstorming such events, it is highly advisable for the PR to check their practicability before sharing them with the client, who will typically be inclined to take the original idea, gold plate it and then stud it with precious jewels. An experienced financial PR once rashly suggested to a client in the UK property sector that it might be possible to induce the US Ambassador to the Court of St James's to attend the 'topping out' of a spectacular new London building with American connections. By the time the client had finished building on this idea the guest of honour was supposed to be greeted by a storm of celebrity tickertape as he arrived in an open Cadillac dressed as Uncle Sam, in a parade headed by a New Orleans jazz band and followed by a troupe of cheerleaders.

Rarely can greater disappointment ever have been etched on a human visage than when the first outline of the idea was shared with the US Embassy in Grosvenor Square and the inevitable words uttered: 'What do you mean, "the Ambassador won't do it?"'

BIDS AND DEALS

This is the big money-earning opportunity for any financial PR, as it is for banks, brokers, accountants, lawyers and any other professional hangers-on who are fortunate enough to be able to obtain a finger-hold on the bandwagon. Despite the ample evidence that takeovers usually destroy shareholder value, they remain popular as a way of providing an even bigger platform for the bidding CEO's burgeoning ego, muddying the waters about the lousy underlying performance of the bidder, and – most importantly – generating millions in fees for the bankers and other advisers who usually dream them up. Even better than that, after a few years they can earn more millions by engineering a demerger when it becomes clear that the combination was, in fact, fatally flawed.

A prime example was a short-lived UK merger of the 1980s involving food and furniture retailing: a combination that had no industrial logic and generated nothing beyond one passable joke: 'I'm not sure about this Asda–MFI business. I bought a chicken yesterday and, before I could even get it home, its legs had dropped off.'

In return for the seven-figure fee a PR must be prepared to endure initial sleeplessness and weeks of unremitting toil. The former because, for reasons no one has ever been able to establish, no bid or deal can be announced without teams of lawyers working through the night and only signing off the necessary documentation in the not-so-early hours. The latter because the bid will proceed to a tediously long, pre-determined and ritualised timetable, rather in the manner of a mediaeval joust. Both sides will have to issue successive appeals to the target's shareholders, and inevitably the bidder will realise at the eleventh hour that the company it is bidding for is worth ever so slightly more than it originally thought.

PRs should beware of overconfidence. On the eve of the Monday morning closure of a bitter inter-brewery takeover battle in the early 2000s, the bidder's PR unaccountably decided to ring around every newspaper in the UK to announce that their client had won. The target's PR, who was having girlfriend troubles at the time, declined to interrupt his weekend by responding to the story, with the result that the story ran unchallenged. Shareholders who were eager to get their hands on the bidder's cash, but did not want to stab the target's management in the back, sat on their hands confident that they would get their money anyway. As a direct result the bidder lost by a whisker, and you may well conclude that it served them right.

BLUFFER'S TIP: *Never underestimate the potential of masterly inactivity to deliver results.*

The PR will be calm and reassuring, adopting a soothing and supportive persona that conceals their inward glee at the 'Kerching!' of crisis management fees that no threatened individual or organisation will even flirt with the idea of pausing to begrudge.

CRISIS COMMUNICATIONS

As nature abhors a vacuum, so the PR adores a crisis. A client will respond to the onset of disaster by turning white, sweating, groaning, wringing their hands and, in extreme cases, suffering a cardiac arrest. The PR, by contrast, will be calm and reassuring, adopting a soothing and supportive persona that conceals their inward glee at the 'Kerching!' of crisis management fees that no threatened individual or organisation will even flirt with the idea of pausing to begrudge.

WHAT CONSTITUTES A CRISIS?

Like an air crash or a major heart attack, it is pretty certain that you will have no difficulty identifying a crisis as soon as you are involved in one, but the following broad guidelines may help:

Death. This covers a broad spectrum from an individual fatality that might not be the client's fault to multiple fatalities that clearly are. The former might only amount to an incident; the later definitely constitutes a crisis. This applies even if the client is in the business of making bullets, missiles or other items clearly designed to kill people because they will self-evidently have failed in their number one mission statement priority of providing 'effective deterrence to ensure that our world-beating products never need to be used'.

Illness. As with death, one person made slightly unwell as the result of, say, mislabelling of a product or insufficiently rigorous temperature control may not quite qualify as a crisis; but multiple individuals made seriously ill most definitely does.

Injury. Serious injury resulting from failures in the design or operation of the client's products or services almost certainly constitutes a crisis even if only one individual is involved, and particularly if said individual is a child.

Accident. A large fire, explosion or oil spillage that qualifies for the appellation 'disaster' clearly constitutes a crisis, regardless of whether client is to blame for it or not.

Cruelty. Mistreatment of animals is likely to be regarded as a crisis by the media, even if it is mistreatment in the course of deliberately killing them to turn them into meat.

Poor customer service. Although we are inured to such everyday suckers of the joy from life as aircraft and trains that never arrive on time, insurance policies that always avoid paying out, self-service tills that never work, call centres that are perennially experiencing 'an unusually high volume of calls', and customer-facing staff who are rude and short-tempered, there comes a tipping point when an organisation's failure to deliver what it promised becomes a full-blown crisis. Examples include the total failure to implement a promised timetable change which results in every train service being cancelled, or a 'too good to be true' offer or competition that results in massive oversubscription and violent crowds besieging the client's stores or other outlets.

IT and logistical failures. If you're in the banking business and your customers can't access their money, that is a crisis. So is running a website and failing to deliver the promised and paid-for goods. Famously, police were called upon to calm the angry British public in 2018 when a fast-food restaurant company's attempt to increase profitability by rationalising distribution led to nationwide shortages of the nation's favourite fried chicken.

Misrepresentation. It was repeatedly emphasised from the outset that the 'Horsegate' meat substitution issues that surfaced in the UK in 2013 had no implications for public health, horsemeat being perfectly edible, but that did not prevent it from being a major crisis that undermined trust in a number of well-known British brands.

Political incorrectness. There used to be a simple rule in PR: 'engage brain before opening mouth'. Now one has to engage all the senses to try to predict the possible offence that might be caused by almost any statement or action, on the grounds that someone somewhere might perceive it to be racist, sexist, transphobic or otherwise offensive.

One of the many malign side-effects of the rise of social media is that it only takes one aggrieved customer, employee or mere passer-by to make an unfavourable observation about a person or organisation's lack of sensitivity on an issue for the whole of the internet to coalesce into a screaming mob, waving pitchforks and demanding retribution.

A communication plan should be prepared, the essence of which will be ensuring that no one in the affected organisation actually speaks to the media and makes the critical mistake of accepting blame for whatever has happened.

HOW TO PREPARE FOR A CRISIS

Follow the old Boy Scout principle:

Do say	Don't say
Be prepared	Dyb dyb dyb dob dob dob*

* Acronym for Do Your Best, Do Our Best, apparently (information that might come in handy for a pub quiz).

Every individual and organisation should undertake regular **risk assessments** that consist, in essence, of repeatedly asking the question 'What could possibly go wrong?'

Having collated the answers, and ideally taken action to eliminate the most obvious risks (e.g. storing plutonium next to the howler monkey enclosure), the designated PR should then prepare a **crisis response plan** with a **template press release** covering all the possible disasters in which the client is most likely to be implicated (in 'delete as applicable' format) plus a catch-all statement expressing regret for the victim(s) and/or their surviving relatives 'at this most difficult time' and promising a 'rigorous investigation' to identify the causes of the problem, with an assurance that 'lessons will be learned'.

A **communication plan** should also be prepared, the essence of which will be ensuring that no one in the affected organisation actually speaks to the media and makes the critical mistake of accepting blame for whatever has happened. All enquiries must instead be channelled to the chosen crisis PR specialist, thus ensuring that it maximises the number of chargeable hours worked on the project.

HOW TO RESPOND TO A CRISIS

There are a number of possible options, which bear a striking resemblance to the five commonly recognised stages of coping with a diagnosis of terminal illness: denial, anger, bargaining, depression and acceptance.

Denial. 'Not our fault, guv'. We took every reasonable precaution to ensure that nothing like this could ever happen – and yet, unaccountably, it did. We are as devastated as those directly affected, who are naturally foremost in our thoughts at this very difficult time.

Anger. Not only was this not our fault, guv, but we are among the victims here. We could never have expected anything like this to happen, and it wouldn't have done without the evil agency of [insert name of perpetrator towards whom the client wishes righteous public anger to be directed].

Bargaining. All right, maybe we are a little bit to blame here – but, really, we did everything we could to prevent it and now we are determined to put things right.

Depression. Oh Christ, we really did screw up, didn't we? I think the CEO himself may have to resign over this one if we are to have any chance of saving the organisation as a whole.

Acceptance. Although I was not directly responsible for the decisions that led to [insert description of catastrophe] I recognise that the buck ultimately stops with me. I have therefore offered my resignation to the board [omit: in the hope that they will refuse to accept it] in order that the organisation may recover under new leadership. I hope that my action will help to safeguard the livelihoods of my many wonderful colleagues [omit: with the obvious exception of those who actually caused this weapons-grade clusterf*ck] and allow the organisation to rebuild and make appropriate recompense to the survivors and families of the victims, who are naturally foremost in my thoughts at this difficult time.

'THE GOLDEN HOUR'

In their ongoing attempt to be considered serious professionals worthy of the same sort of respect as specialists working in A&E, the PR will naturally emphasise the importance of responding to the fatality/incident/outrage/tweet as quickly as possible, before the bandwagon with the scythes attached to the wheels, intent on mowing down reputation and management alike, can really get rolling. This means having the **communication plan**, the **template press release** and the **agreed senior communicator** all in place and ready to be deployed. The bluffer will assume a look of distant piety when talking about 'the golden hour' in which it is vital to wheel all of the above into action. Sound principles here are to communicate what you definitely know, try to find out what you don't know as quickly as you can, stick to facts rather than speculation, and clearly set out what the client is doing to address the issue.

NB 'Sticking to the facts' does not include telling the media that the CEO won't be able to answer their questions about the tragic death on the ghost train because he is spending the day grouse shooting on a remote moor with no mobile signal.

Two practical examples of crisis management
How to do it: Tylenol. No chapter on crisis management would be complete without a mention of Tylenol, the

best-selling US analgesic. In 1982 seven people died in the Chicago area after swallowing capsules of Extra-Strength Tylenol that had been laced with cyanide by an unidentified maniac. The owners Johnson & Johnson responded quickly in issuing warnings, recalling 31 million bottles of the product and offering to replace these capsules with solid tablets free of charge, before relaunching the capsules in tamper-proof packaging. The episode cost the company $100 million but it emerged with its reputation intact. Unsurprisingly this has become widely cited as the model response to a crisis: take charge and do it quickly in order to retain the public's trust.

How not to do it: BP. When BP's Deepwater Horizon oil rig exploded in 2010, killing 11 workers and causing a massive oil spill in the Gulf of Mexico that ranked as one of the greatest environmental disasters in US history, the company did its utmost to stem the leak and fund the clean-up. Unfortunately the company's CEO, while expressing regret for the damage, also allowed his personal interest to intrude with the words 'There's no one who wants this thing over more than I do, I'd like my life back.' It cost him his job and furnishes this valuable lesson for every CEO in any future crisis: always remember that it's not about you (for once), it's about the people your organisation has affected.

In a crisis, as in all other situations, never lose sight of the Second Rule of PR:

If in doubt, say nowt.

MEDIA RELATIONS

The PR professional has one key advantage over most ordinary mortals: he or she is not afraid of journalists. In many cases this will be because they have previously been employed as journalists themselves. Or if not, because they have met enough journalists to know that hacks are not, by and large, 'out to get you' or deliberately to misrepresent what you say. They merely do so with such alarming regularity out of laziness or incompetence rather than malice.

HOW TO COMMUNICATE WITH THE MEDIA

In the olden days it was very easy: simply walk into the pub nearest to a newspaper office (often adorned with a helpful name like 'The Printer's Pie'), approach the drunkest-looking person at the bar and ask if they might be interested in a story.

A key part of the journalist's skills in those days was the ability to remember things learned when very, very drunk. Males could take advantage of regular visits to the lavatory to press their foreheads on the refreshingly cold tiles above the urinal and scribble key facts in their trusty notebooks.

Another key skill was the ability to decipher important facts scrawled in notebooks when very, very drunk.

The regrettable rise of sobriety, the decline of print, the growth of the internet and the move from one daily (or weekly) deadline to constant updating of online stories has sadly done for this old approach, but one vestige of the Victorian age remains:

The press release

More than 30 years ago PR old hands were pointing out that the term 'press release' was outmoded, because they now addressed a much wider and more diverse media audience than the press. However, attempted innovations such as calling the thing a 'news release' instead never caught on.

The ideal press release should communicate something that is actually worth knowing, and should do so via:

1. **An eye-catching headline**, ideally incorporating the key piece of information contained in the release.
2. **A pithy opening par** (journalists always call a paragraph a 'par'; a 'para' is someone who jumps out of aeroplanes with hostile intent) conveying the nub of the story.
3. **A fuller second par** adding useful supporting information.
4. **A memorable quote** from the egomaniac client on whose behalf the release has been issued, that will make them appear to be a towering genius.

The distribution list

Having constructed your press release, the next thing is to get it into the hands of the media. There are many companies trying to make a living out of selling up-to-date media databases that will enable you to target the titles and individuals most likely to be interested in your latest missive. Keeping track of all those who leave journalism for PR each month must indeed be a full-time job. Alternatively you could just Google (other search engines are available) the subject of your release, and/or the geographical area in which you are most interested, and assemble an appropriate list yourself. Or, if you are feeling particularly lazy, just send it to a few of your mates and hope for the best.

Once upon a time getting a piece of news into the papers presented as many challenges as a game of what used to be called Chinese whispers.

The EU's General Data Protection Regulation (GDPR – also interpretable as God Damn PRs) might be expected to make it more difficult to target hapless individuals with unwanted crap headed with the words 'press release'. However, the bluffer should be able to affect an attitude of supreme nonchalance in arguing that they are sending the information to their targets in their professional capacities, not as private individuals, and are therefore not covered by the regulation. And that, M'Lud, concludes the case for the defence.

How to send it?

There is a short answer to this: by email.

Once upon a time getting a piece of news into the papers presented as many challenges as a game of what used to be called Chinese whispers, before this became unacceptable for reasons of political correctness.

First the PR would sketch out their thoughts in actual handwriting, or dictate them if pretentiously inclined that way. Many a laugh was generated in olde worlde PR offices through the double entendre implicit in the question, 'Can I use your Dictaphone?'

Then the PR would have their manuscript or tape typed up by an amanuensis. Once approved, the release would almost certainly have to be retyped on a stencil to allow it to be printed for distribution. Teams of highly motivated messengers would then speed the release to the desks of the targeted hacks, where the release would be woozily read through a haze of cigarette smoke and alcohol and, if it had sufficient appeal, a story might be banged out on a manual typewriter, altered by a sub-editor and ultimately set in hot metal for printing in a newspaper.

Given the scope for errors to be introduced each time the information was rekeyed, it should occasion little surprise that there was often a considerable difference between the original germ of an idea and the story that finally appeared in the paper.

Modern technology has eliminated most of these stages, and the jobs that went with them. Now the PR typically composes the release on a word processor and distributes it by email direct to the journalist, who will – if it is deemed worthy – simply cut and paste selected extracts and send it off to print. The potential for both entertaining and embarrassing errors is thereby much reduced.

The embargo

There are two possible reasons for placing an embargo on a press release, forbidding the publication of its contents before a designated date and time:

1. The subject covered is of an immensely complex or technical nature, making it sensible to allow all journalists some time to digest and fully comprehend it before they commit the story to print.

2. The client and/or PR wishes to take advantage of an expected lull in media activity, and is too lazy to work during that lull themselves. Thus they might send out a release on a Friday embargoed for 00.01 on the following Bank Holiday Monday, hoping that there will be sod all else to write about then, and that no one will interrupt their weekends by ringing up with awkward questions on Saturday or Sunday.

The exclusive

There are five sorts of exclusive story in the media, ranked in order of their probability with the likeliest first:

1. The story obtained by breaking an embargo (q.v.).

2. The story given by a PR to the news outlet they deem to be most interested in the subject, or the most influential, in the knowledge that doing so will make enemies of all the chosen outlet's rivals.

3. The story obtained through an egomaniac client's failure to heed their PR's simple instruction to utter the words 'off the record' before voicing some clearly

libellous remarks about their competitors or the political establishment.

4. In financial bids and deals, the story leaked by a banker eager to demonstrate how clever and important they are. Financial PRs are the least likely participant in any transaction to leak the story, thereby overturning weeks of careful planning for its dissemination. They are, however, much the most likely to be saddled with the blame.

5. The story obtained through fearless and diligent journalistic work exploring an issue of genuine public interest, overcoming all obstacles erected by politicians, the military-industrial complex, and PRs.

The follow-up

As previously noted, having circulated their release by email, many PRs feel compelled to 'reach out' to journalists to check that they have received it, ask whether they have any questions about it, and obtain an early indication of how likely their story is to feature on the next day's front page.

This is a fantastically unpopular course of action among its overburdened media recipients, but this knowledge must be weighed against the fact that the fee-paying client naturally expects the PR to make slightly more effort than pressing 'send' on an email.

In these circumstances, the bluffer will tell the client that they did absolutely everything they could, including speaking to all the journalists potentially interested in the story. So long as you don't specify **when** you spoke to them this might even be true.

'Off the record'

In conducting media relations, it is of the utmost importance that both PR and client understand the meaning of those valuable phrases 'non-attributable' and 'off the record'.

A non-attributable statement is one which the journalist is free to report, even quoting the exact words used, but may not attribute to the person who said them. An off the record statement is an utterance even more deeply mired in obscurity, in that it literally cannot be recorded or reproduced, even in paraphrase; its prime purpose is to steer the journalist in the right direction without leaving the client's fingerprints anywhere on the resulting story.

Understanding these key terms, and the difference between them, will greatly increase the bluffer's chances of being mistaken for a PR expert.

Clearly, the value of making a comment non-attributable or off the record may be questionable if the words are uttered in the course of a long interview in which most of the rest of the content is presented as direct quotations from the subject of the resulting profile. They are also not things that may be invoked retrospectively, e.g. 'When I said just now that my predecessor as CEO was an incompetent crook who should be jailed for fiddling the accounts and bestiality – that was off the record.'

Since most CEOs are ticking time bombs of resentments, with a host of scores to settle, the PR needs to be alert at all times for the signs that they are about to go off on one, and to assert 'this is non-attributable'/'off the record' if they do not have the force of character or adequate inspiration simply to alter the direction of the conversation.

Economy with the actualité

No PR who wishes to have a long and successful career can hope to do so by lying outright to the media. However, that does not mean that it is necessary to blurt out everything the PR knows about a sensitive subject as soon as it is raised with them. The PR should focus carefully on what the journalist is actually asking, respond only to that point, and await supplementary questions with due care and attention.

The courtroom oath	The PR's oath
I swear that the evidence that I shall give, shall be the truth, the whole truth and nothing but the truth, so help me God.	I shall tell the truth and nothing but the truth, though not necessarily the whole truth. Please God, help me.

If the journalist has received a clearly well-informed tip-off that Company A is about to launch a takeover bid for Company B, or that Celebrity C is about to be the subject of divorce proceedings because of his or her affair with Celebrity D, there is no point in denying outright that these are going to happen.

However, it may be perfectly possible – and indeed true – in the first instance that negotiations are at an extremely delicate stage and that premature exposure in the media might result in the deal not taking place after all (a self-unfulfilling prophecy); or in the second instance that reconciliation might yet be possible if only the distress of a front page splash could be avoided – and won't you please think of the children?

The outcome may be a fruitful and mutually beneficial negotiation in which the journalist agrees to hold back from publicising the story on the promise of exclusivity once the PR is in a position to confirm that the takeover/divorce is definitely going ahead.

Although any PR who agrees such a deal and then fails to deliver it should consider themselves a dead man walking and start looking for alternative employment as soon as possible.

The non-denial denial

This device has become regrettably popular as an alternative way out of the sort of tricky situation outlined above. The PR makes (or, more likely, recommends to the client) a bold and apparently unambiguous denial of a proposition which, on forensically close examination, proves not to deny it at all. Though usually that only becomes clear after the proposition has, in fact, been proven correct.

For example:

Day 1:

Journalist: *Is your client planning to close its Grange Moor widget factory, throwing 500 people out of work?*

PR: *That is the most ridiculous suggestion I have ever heard!*

Journalist: *So you are denying that it is true?*

PR: *I am stating that my client has no plans to close its Grange Moor widget factory.*

Journalist: *Are you sure?*

PR: *Yes.*

Journalist: *OK.*

Day 10: Client announces the opening of a consultation on the possible closure of its Grange Moor widget factory that might lead to up to 495 compulsory redundancies.

Journalist: *You bastard!*

PR: *I said the client had no plans to close it, and they didn't at the time we spoke. It's a consultation and there may be no redundancies, and in any case there won't be 500. Also it would have been wrong to upset the workforce with premature speculation.*

Journalist: *I know where you live.*

PR: *That is the most ridiculous suggestion I have ever heard!* Etc.

TELEVISION AND RADIO

Broadcast media may be addressed with the same (inaccurately titled) release as newspapers, also known as 'the dead tree press', but they have additional needs. In particular, television requires moving images to fill the void while the client burbles on about their latest triumph in the background, since viewers are less likely to switch channels if given the chance to look at something more interesting than a middle-aged white man talking about himself. For historic reasons, these pre-prepared assemblies of extra footage are called B-rolls, distinguishing them from the A-roll of main footage. Neither term has any practical relevance now that actual film is no longer cut and spliced, but B-roll lives on as handy descriptive shorthand for the supplementary material supplied by PRs to broadcasters.

'Have you remembered to do the B-roll?'

Do say	Don't say
Yes, we've intercut the cute pussy cat in the kitchen window with the hungry orphans in the rainforest and it all looks great.	Yes, I put a new one in this morning. And before you ask, I flushed and washed my hands as well.

THE DIGITAL WORLD

The World Wide Web is now central to the life of every person on the planet with access to electrical power and a telephone line, and therefore to the work of every PR. This creates a huge range of bothersome but profitable opportunities including the creation and constant updating of:

THE AGENCY WEBSITE

Where once a PR agency might have relied upon a slickly produced brochure or video, or simply positive word of mouth, to generate new client leads, its website is now the main window in which it must display its wares to tempt unwary passers-by – whether they be potential clients or possible employees.

Naturally the agency will wish to make itself stand out from its peers through the use of striking imagery and a range of blindingly impressive case studies illustrative of its work. Though it appears that anyone can write the copy for an agency website by simply juggling the following words:

Agency website buzzword bingo				
Integrated	Passionate	Intelligent	Engagement	Innovative
Leading	Global	Reputation	Go-to	Experienced
Smart	Strategic	Insight	Sustainability	Award-winning
Creative	Influential	Vision	Value	Different

In today's highly competitive market agencies appear to be falling over themselves to look more serious and successful than any other, and the concept of PR work as fun has sadly evaporated. It is almost certainly impermissible to feel nostalgic for the early days of the internet, when the agency's creative director might take a long drag on his spliff and drawl, 'I've got a great idea for the site. Let's get the whole team drunk paintballing in the nude.'

As well as maintaining a constant watch for new buzzwords to keep the website thrillingly up to date, the PR must keep track of … promotions through the dizzying array of titles which make the rank structure of the Ruritanian armed forces seem comically primitive.

As well as maintaining a constant watch for new buzzwords to keep the website thrillingly up to date, the PR must keep track of personnel turnover and constantly adjust the website to reflect not only arrivals and departures, but promotions through the dizzying array of titles, which make the rank structure of the Ruritanian armed forces seem comically primitive. These titles should include (though need not be restricted to) account executive, associate director, director, creative director, marketing director, digital director, consultant, senior consultant, partner, senior partner, chief executive, chairman and founder.

THE CLIENT WEBSITE

No self-respecting client will have just one website. If it is engaged in the production of items smaller than aircraft carriers or nuclear reactors, it will most likely have an ecommerce site, attempting to sell its wares to trade customers and/or the public at large. Then there will doubtless be a corporate website, extolling the brilliance of the organisation's strategy and management. Either as offshoots of this, or as standalone websites, it will wish to wax lyrical about the glamorous career opportunities it offers, its rock solid commitment to Corporate Social Responsibility, and its wonderful work for charity. If a public company, or a private one with traded bonds or other securities, it will also require a section or entire site dedicated to investor relations.

All of the above offer rich opportunities for the PR, who will not only play a central role in devising the key messages for these sites, but will also need to ensure that they are kept constantly updated: a task so monumentally and mind-numbingly boring that it defies description or comparison, particularly since they started applying long-life paint to the Forth Rail Bridge.

The bad news is that the work cannot be ignored, as

almost the only people who ever read corporate websites are single-issue obsessives with an axe to grind. The good news is that the long list of people who never read them almost certainly includes the client's entire senior management team, so that they are never likely to be able to query the huge number of hours the PR claims to have expended in keeping the site entirely shipshape.

SOCIAL MEDIA FEEDS

There are alleged to be some 200 different social media platforms in existence at the time of writing, but the ones on which both agency and client are likely to wish to focus are Facebook and Twitter. The former facilitates longer posts and slower burning conversations; exchanges on the latter tend to be nasty, brutish and short.

Let us illustrate this with an example of responses to a member of the public spotting a product offer on the front page of their daily newspaper first thing in the morning, then going to a branch of the retailer concerned late in the afternoon and discovering that it had sold out.

Facebook vs Twitter

Facebook	Twitter
I was very disappointed on visiting your Bullocks Wood store today to find that you did not have any of the Hann Miracle Rejuvenating Serum specially reduced to 50p, as advertised on the front page of the *Bullocks Wood Bugle* this morning.	Everyone boycott these frauds! No 50p Hann's Serum in Bullocks Wood this morning!

Facebook	Twitter
We are very sorry for your disappointment, but our advert did make it clear that there was limited availability of the product.	*We are very sorry for your disappointment, but our advert did make it clear that there was limited availability of the product.*
Yes, but surely you should have had enough in each store to satisfy expected demand before deciding to advertise it?	Bollocks – this is outright fraud. As I'd expect from a company whose chairman is a racist tax evader and suspected paedophile.
We took reasonable steps to assess likely demand before advertising, and the advert did clearly state 'when it's gone, it's gone'. We stock a wide range of other miracle rejuvenating serums at competitive prices.	*We took reasonable steps to assess likely demand before advertising, and the advert did clearly state 'when it's gone, it's gone'. We stock a wide range of other miracle rejuvenating serums at competitive prices.*
Yes, but I had set my heart on the 50p Hann serum and went to a lot of trouble and expense to get to the store, and feel that you should compensate me for my disappointment.	No excuses! I demand compensation or I'm going to the press with your CEO's dirty little secret.
We value your custom but cannot offer compensation for our inability to supply what we made clear was a product in limited supply.	*Please DM us urgently.*

Facebook	Twitter
Did you ever actually have some of the 50p Serum in Bullocks Wood or were you practising a cynical deception to lure me and other customers into your store in the hope that we would buy something more expensive?	It's too late for that now!
We can confirm that we had an average stock of more than 10 jars of the product in every store across the company.	*Please DM us urgently.*
Yes, but how many did you actually have in Bullocks Wood?	Never, ever shop with this company – they are lying, thieving, perverted cultural appropriators.
Owing to a delivery issue that was beyond our control, the Bullocks Wood store had a lower than average stock of the product at the start of trading yesterday.	*Please DM us urgently.*
How many, exactly?	Also their stores are crap, their staff are rude and their products are shit.
A child ran in front of our lorry and, although she escaped with minor injuries, our driver was severely traumatised and unable to complete his deliveries.	*Please follow us so that we may DM you.*
How many, exactly?	Never! Why would I want to follow the worst retailer in the world?

Facebook	Twitter
None, but this was wholly exceptional within the company and was due to circumstances completely beyond our control.	*We would like to make you an offer to allay your disappointment.*
I had a wasted journey and feel entitled to demand compensation.	I have followed you.
OK, send us your postal address and we will mail you a bottle of Hann's Serum with our compliments.	*DM: please send us your postal address and we will mail you a bottle of Hann's Serum with our compliments.*
Make it two.	DM: Make it two.
Done.	*DM: Done.*

REVIEW WEBSITES

It is said that a good review on a website like TripAdvisor can make a business – particularly a small one – and a seriously bad review can certainly break one. The owners of such sites assert that rigorous measures are in place to prevent abuse of their facilities, so the popular conviction that most of the ecstatic five star raves are posted by employees or friends of the proprietor, and most of the one-star slatings by competitors and personal enemies, must clearly be incorrect. However, even if there is no role for the PR in dreaming up and posting fake reviews, there is certainly one in composing grovelling responses to the more damning assessments of establishments. These are generally agreed to afford a superior PR solution to negative comments, though they are vastly less entertaining than the angry, alcohol-fuelled rants typically posted late in the evening by aggrieved hoteliers and restaurateurs in person.

Politicisation of communications is visible around the globe, not least through the constantly revolving door of the Trump White House.

PUBLIC AFFAIRS

AIMS AND PURPOSE

Once upon a time there was a rather murky and faintly disreputable practice known as lobbying; now there is a growing and highly respectable industry calling itself public affairs. This is the branch of PR concerned with communicating the aims and desires of individuals, businesses, trade bodies, charities and campaigners to political audiences. In the UK alone, these comprise the national government, devolved administrations in Scotland, Wales and Northern Ireland (when the last is actually functioning), regional and local government (including elected mayoralties, metropolitan boroughs, county and district councils), individual Members of Parliament and the House of Lords, and the various committees of both Houses, together with the media diaspora associated with all of the above: the well-established Lobby group of Parliamentary journalists working for both traditional and new digital media outlets; venerable primarily political magazines like *The Spectator* and *New Statesman*; broadcast political discussion programmes and podcasts; political think tanks; party political websites; and so on and so forth.

No wonder the seasoned and polished public affairs professional is able to charge so much for their ability to influence such a diverse, highly educated and powerful audience.

That influence will usually be exercised in two main arenas:

Policy: Attempting to persuade those in power to accommodate the specific best interests of the client in the framing of primary legislation, statutory instruments or local by-laws.

Reputation: Endeavouring to 'big up' the client as a hugely reputable and important individual or organisation that should be consulted as a matter of course on all major issues.

If, say, the client is a brewer of alcoholic beverages, its public affairs adviser will work assiduously to convince Parliamentarians and senior officials that the client is deeply responsible in its approach; would never countenance the advertising or sale of its products to minors; does all in its power to discourage excessive consumption, resulting anti-social behaviour and associated policing and healthcare costs; promotes diversity in all its operations; and naturally makes a major contribution to employment, duty and tax revenues, and to the country's balance of payments through its flourishing export trade.

The adviser will seek both to promote the continuation

of existing policies which are to the advantage of the client, and to discourage any changes of direction which might prove potentially damaging – such as, say, requiring alcoholic beverages to be sold in plain packaging with the legend **'ALCOHOL CAUSES CANCER: DRINK THIS AND YOU WILL DIE'** printed across it in large bold print.

At the same time, public affairs practitioners working for lightly disguised temperance organisations will be promoting precisely the opposite approach. Because not all politicians are entirely stupid, a convention has developed in recent years whereby they do not simply tell the voting public things they know we do not want to hear, such as that we are all (on average) too fat, too lazy and much too addicted to strong drink. Instead they supply the funding to 'charities' which then 'lobby' them to take action on all these fronts.

Now, when they wreck your favourite soft drink or cereal by leaning on manufacturers to remove most of the sugar from it, or arbitrarily slash the recommended maximum weekly alcohol intake and suggest that the only safe way to proceed is total abstinence, they can adopt an innocent face and claim that they were only buckling to intense pressure from disinterested 'campaigners'.

WHICH SIDE TO BE ON?

In deciding whether to practise public affairs on behalf of the evil capitalist drink manufacturer or the worthy health-promoting charity, you will no doubt be influenced primarily by your own convictions and conscience. If you tend to favour well-cut suits and enjoy a fine malt whisky, it is reasonable to deduce that you will be happier in the former camp. If you knit your own clothes from self-woven vegan-friendly artificial fibres, you'll probably fit right in at the campaigning charity.

Were you to be the sort of unprincipled individual who is primarily concerned with maximising their own income and profile, the corporation would also be a wiser choice.

If contemplating a career in public affairs that involves actually working for a political party, conscience must once more be your guide. Though for those with fluid convictions, it may be worth reflecting that the governing party has all the resources of the State at its disposal, while the opposition (whoever it may be) is much less well endowed with funds and manpower, and hence eager to employ cheap, keen, young people who may reasonably expect to learn a lot in a relatively short time, advance up the career ladder more rapidly, and quite possibly sleep with some moderately interesting and influential people in the process.

Working for the opposition also provides adrenalin-boosting and ultimately skill- and career-enhancing experience in working under extreme pressure. As, for example, when the Leader of the Opposition has to be briefed on how to respond credibly to a Budget speech he has only just heard. True, all important details will almost certainly have been leaked to the newspapers over the previous weekend, but it is important to check for actual delivery in case any have been dropped or modified in the face of popular protest or derision.

WORKING IN GOVERNMENT

Like the old-fashioned in-house PR person in the corporate sector, 'press officers' in government were traditionally career civil servants who had, perhaps, proven unsuitable for more stellar roles. For those above a certain age in the UK, the defining memory is of the Ministry of Defence spokesman during the 1982 Falklands War, who made his name by delivering bad news very sonorously and incredibly slowly (for the benefit of reporters taking dictation in traditional notebooks).

It is doubtful whether anyone will ever surpass the PR mastery of the Iraqi minister dubbed 'Comical Ali' for his sterling efforts to present the war of 2003 as an unalloyed triumph for the regime of Saddam Hussein, even as advancing enemy tanks could be observed trundling up behind him.

All this changed in the white heat of the Blair revolution from 1997, which drove huge growth in the numbers of politically appointed Special Advisers (SPADs) and saw them propelled into the key positions of head of communications at both 10 Downing Street and the Treasury. The memoirs of Alastair Campbell (press secretary to Tony Blair) and Damian McBride (special adviser to Gordon Brown) afford valuable insights into the techniques they employed to advance the interests of their respective bosses.

Similar politicisation of communications is visible around the globe, not least through the constantly revolving door of the Trump White House. However, it is doubtful whether anyone will ever surpass the PR mastery of the Iraqi minister dubbed 'Comical Ali' for his sterling efforts to present the war of 2003 as an unalloyed triumph for the regime of Saddam Hussein, even as advancing enemy tanks could be observed trundling up behind him. It is safe to say that, despite his astonishing chutzpah, he should not be viewed as a role model for aspiring bluffers.

WORKING FOR ROYALTY

Those with a taste for grand uniforms and decorations, palatial surroundings and the distant prospect of a gong to offset years of low wages may wish to consider the possibility of working for the Royal family. (Naturally by 'the' Royal family we mean the British one, though other royal families are available.) In the UK, each household has its own PR complement and any candidate will need to evaluate whether it is better to be working for someone universally respected, even loved, but with a limited life expectancy; or for someone with decades ahead of them who, it is alleged, does not enjoy quite the same level of affection among the household staff.

Do say	Don't say
Ma'am to rhyme with jam	Ma'am to rhyme with smarm

INTEGRATION

After 'award-winning', 'integrated' is perhaps the most popular buzzword to be found on PR company websites.

Like the man in the showroom seeking to persuade you to buy a whole new fitted kitchen when you only popped in to pick up a replacement door handle for one of the cupboards, the smooth PR salesperson will emphasise the value of public affairs as part of a total, seamless package designed to boost the profile and credibility of the client across the full spectrum of consumer, media, financial and political audiences. Cultivating all these contacts will prove invaluable when, for example, the public affairs division is able to rope in a Parliamentary Under-Secretary of State to lend their name to a supportive quote about a consumer-friendly initiative that is also calculated to boost the client's profits and hence its value to investors.

SPECIALISATION

There are also opportunities within the broad realm of public affairs for specialisation: for example in the fields of planning or licensing. The planning consultant is the genius who can potentially turn your five-acre patch of mud into a metaphorical goldmine, by securing the necessary consents to turn it into a high-density housing development, wind or solar farm, opencast coal mine, nuclear waste dump or fracking hub. This will involve exercising his or her considerable powers of persuasion on the local authority's planners and councillors, and on those higher up the political food chain, as NIMBYs and environmentalists object furiously to the destruction of the patch of land about which, in truth, nobody much cared until someone proposed to do something more profitable with it.

Luckily the dice are permanently weighted in favour of developers because, funds permitting, they can always object to a refusal of planning permission until it reaches the desk of the Secretary of State – and even beyond that if they are prepared to have recourse to the courts. Those on the other side, however, have no opportunity to object to a grant of planning permission unless the local authority's decision was so manifestly perverse as to justify legal action against it. Rather as the IRA observed at the time of the Brighton bomb, the developer only has to be lucky once; the opponents of development have to be lucky all the time.

REGISTRATION

If you wish to employ a public affairs consultant you will clearly be looking for one that is entirely reputable and unlikely to drag your name through the mud by handing out brown envelopes stuffed with used banknotes to likely Parliamentary helpers. Fortunately help is at hand in the form of registers of lobbyists. Unfortunately this is one field yet to see the benefits of integration. The UK alone possesses a statutory Register of Consultant Lobbyists, established under the snappily titled Transparency of Lobbying, Non-Party Campaigning and Trade Union Administration Act 2014; an official Scottish register established under the Lobbying (Scotland) Act 2016; a 'universal, voluntary' Lobbying Register established in 2015 by the Chartered Institute of Public Relations (CIPR); and a register of 'political practitioners and their clients' maintained by the Association of Professional Political Consultants (APPC). At the time of writing the members of the APPC were fighting like cats in a sack over their leaders' proposals to merge the organisation with the CIPR. It almost seemed, to an outside observer, as though they might be in need of some PR advice.

THE SORDID TOPICS OF MONEY AND STATUS

CAN YOU MAKE A FORTUNE IN PR?

Yes, if you are exceptionally creative and diligent, or outstandingly lucky. Though the easiest way to make a small fortune in PR, as in most callings, is to have inherited a large one before starting out.

According to the 2018 *Sunday Times Rich List* (admittedly not necessarily the most reliable of sources, since it has been known to accept the wild claims of PRs without too much questioning), Sir Alan Parker, the founder of Brunswick PR in the UK, has accumulated wealth of £138m from his endeavours. It will not have escaped the attention of socially conscious readers that he has also acquired a knighthood, awarded in 2014 for 'services to business, charitable giving and philanthropy' at a time when, surely entirely coincidentally, his friend and confidant David Cameron was Prime Minister.

(The United Kingdom tends to honour those who have made lots of money only if they make a respectable pretence of being eager to give away at least some of it.)

Sir Alan's counterpart Roland Rudd, founder of Finsbury PR, reportedly made £40m when he sold the business to the WPP advertising conglomerate in 2001, and continues to jog along on a mere £3m p.a. as Finsbury's chairman.

Both of these gentlemen, far from coincidentally, made their fortunes in financial PR, where multi-million pound fees to PRs have become commonplace in major transactions, and may even look reasonable in the context of the stratospheric sums pocketed by those slightly higher up the advisory hierarchy: investment, bankers, brokers, corporate lawyers and accountants.

The undisputed genius of Sir Alan and Mr Rudd, and many others holding senior PR positions in the UK and elsewhere, has been to transform the PR from the mere 'press agent' – the red-faced, pinstriped bod who waited outside the boardroom to receive the agreed announcement and arrange its distribution to the media, making him little more than a posh messenger boy – into a key member of the senior advisory team, helping to frame the messages from the outset.

Both are past masters of 'networking': Sir Alan famously contrived to be close to both Gordon Brown and David Cameron, even lending the latter his house when an unexpected item in the European referendum bagging area led to the Camerons' ejection from their tied cottage in Downing Street in 2016.

Both also illustrate the theory that the best way

to make a large amount of money in PR is to set up a business and then either retain it (Parker) or sell it on to some other mug (Rudd). The snag with the second option being that the value of the firm remains highly dependent on the founder's continuing participation. At the very least, any sane purchaser will demand an 'earn-out' ensuring that the vendor's contacts and skills remain at its disposal for several years to come.

At which point the founder will either decamp to their chosen beach to sip pina coladas or, more likely, attempt to replicate their past success by founding another PR business.

TITLES

Quite apart from Sir Alan's knighthood, PR boasts an array of grand and euphemistic titles that would surely impress even the Habsburg court of the mid-19th century. Those such as Partner, Director and Account Executive, previously noted, are dully obvious. But why employ a receptionist when you could appoint a Director of First Impressions, or a teaboy when you could add a Chief Hospitality Officer to the payroll? Director of Storytelling, Chief Creative Officer, Brand Ambassador, Senior Happiness Co-ordinator, Social Media Guru, Powerpoint Wizard and even Client Experience Ninja are just some of the possibilities waiting to be snapped up – though perhaps the finest example yet, discovered on Twitter in mid-2018, is 'Journalist Success Manager'.

Luckily no one who is anyone in PR these days carries anything as old-fashioned as a business card, recipients of which would naturally be inclined to translate all of the above as 'tosser'.

REMUNERATION

Is PR well paid? Well, it's paid, and according to the UK CIPR 'State of the Profession' [sic] survey in 2018, practitioners may expect to earn an average salary of £24,223 at age 16–24 and £73,613 if they stay the course until age 55–64. Amazingly, UK salaries tend to increase with experience and, generally speaking, proximity to London. Less predictably perhaps, those working in-house in the private sector earn more on average than those performing the same role in the public sector or working for agencies (though this average may be dragged down by single-person consultancies paying themselves mainly in free gin and Twiglets). Unsurprisingly, Chartered Practitioners earn the highest pay of all.

In no circumstances will bluffers allow themselves to give way to even the slightest hint of a feeling that they may be pursuing an inherently ridiculous and often futile profession.

These averages may not make the blood race compared with the rewards available to chief executives, stockbrokers, broadcasting personalities or professional footballers. But PR offers safe (though not necessarily secure) and relatively undemanding indoor work that assuredly beats digging the roads, picking fruit, mining, deep-sea diving or steeplejacking.

RESPECT

Yes, but will people respect me for being a PR? Short answer: no, but organisations like the CIPR are working hard at it, particularly towards securing PR its proper recognition as a 'strategic management discipline'. Apparently the main obstacle to this is that people think that PR is all about copywriting, editing and media relations rather than high-level strategic planning. The only snag with the programme is that their own research indicates that even the most senior people in PR actually spend the bulk of their time on, er, copywriting, editing and media relations.

In no circumstances will bluffers allow themselves to be deterred by this, or give way to even the slightest hint of a feeling that they may be pursuing an inherently ridiculous and often futile profession. Rather, they will redouble their efforts to secure the respect they deserve, perhaps even devoting their limited spare time to writing widely unread books on the subject.

ß

There's no point in pretending that you know everything about PR – nobody does – but if you've got this far and absorbed at least a modicum of the information and advice contained within these pages, then you will almost certainly know more than 99% of the rest of the human race about why PR exists, how it developed, and what it aims to achieve. Oh, and about why everybody working in it feels so massively undervalued.

What you now do with this information is up to you, but here's a suggestion: be confident about your newfound knowledge, see how far it takes you, but above all have fun using it. You are now a bona fide expert in the art of bluffing about a subject that provides a livelihood for more bluffers than almost any other, with the possible exceptions of marketing, politics and quantum physics.

And remember: if in doubt, say nowt.

GLOSSARY

Term	Media meaning	PR meaning	Client meaning
Above the fold	Top half of broadsheet page	Prime positioning of story achieved by us	Somewhere on the hill beyond the sheep pen
Back bench	Senior journalists	Junior MPs	Supportive furniture
Banner	Large advert across top of page	Placard that requires two people to hold it	What broadcasters should do to left-wing female MPs
Berliner	Mid-sized newspaper, between tabloid and broadsheet	Resident of Berlin	Type of iced doughnut
Blogger	Idiot amateur who writes free of charge	Potentially important influencer	Second-class lumberjack

Term	Media meaning	PR meaning	Client meaning
Blurb	Descriptive introduction to writer	Advertising copy	Geordie condom
Breaking news	Important unplanned story	Unexpected disruption to careful PR planning/ opportunity to bury bad news	Irritant that might interfere with lunch or golf
Broadsheet	Traditional large press format	Posh newspaper	Super Kingsize
Byline	Name of person who wrote the story	Name of person who followed our briefing	Rural branch railway
Caption	Text describing an illustration	Carefully chosen words to add impact to a photograph	Thingy to which one's yacht is moored
Churnalism	The worst sort of journalism, mindlessly regurgitating press releases	The best sort of journalism, mindlessly regurgitating press releases	Journalism pronounced after a half decent lunch
Circulation	Number of copies of a title sold or given away	Massively inflated figure for people reached by any PR initiative	Blood supply

Term	Media meaning	PR meaning	Client meaning
City desk	UK: team covering business stories US: team covering local stories	Team about to come and work in financial PR for vastly increased salaries	Opposite of country desk
Client	Posh sort of customer	Egomaniac bill-payer	Much misunderstood individual doing their best
Columnist	Author of regular opinion column, increasingly unpaid	Influencer under our influence	Marxist
Correction	Something we will do our utmost to avoid printing	Something we can threaten to demand in the hope of eliciting a favour	Small downward movement in share price that is all for the best, really
Credit	Attribution, particularly of photograph	Something for which we constantly strive	Something the wise person never gives
Crosshead	Words used to break up blocks of text	Mysterious part of an internal combustion engine	Angry school leader
Deadline	Time for submission of copy	Vague target, usually breached	Big words at the top of the page

Term	Media meaning	PR meaning	Client meaning
Editor	Big boss	Prime target for schmoozing	Someone in journalism who is too grand to write anything themselves
Em	Measure of print size	Intern so called to avoid confusion with colleague named Emma	Useful word to know for Scrabble
Embargoed	Great opportunity for an exclusive	Story that can't be published until we say so	Small town near Abergavenny
Exclusive	Story that appears nowhere else	Carefully manipulated placement	A place with a high bar to entry; my club
Feature	Longer article	Key promise in all new business pitches	Centrepiece of house, garden or estate; perhaps a folly
Font	Typeface style	Handy substitute for swear word	Thing used for christenings
Freelance	Journalist who is not on the staff	Invaluable substitute for actual paid journalist	Unpaid jouster
Gutter	Space between facing pages	Burning unsteadily, like our reputation	Rainwater collector
Headline	Main title	Thing not written by the journalist we briefed, hence not our fault	Much the most important thing about any article ever published

Term	Media meaning	PR meaning	Client meaning
Hi-res	Quality of photo required for print reproduction	Hyphen unfortunately placed in 'hires'	That place where we go skiing in Colorado?
Leader	Editorial opinion piece	Something we aspire to influence	Me
Libel	Untrue defamatory statement, which we are terrified of making	Something we'd dearly like the media to print about our clients' rivals	Thing that shows the address on a parcel
Masthead	Main title of publication	Where we run the idea flag up to, to see whether anyone salutes	Top bit of my yacht
Off the record	Information we will publish without revealing our source	Something the client did not mean to say, but we cannot deny	All clear to blurt out anything I like
Orphan	Opening line of paragraph placed at the end of a column of text	Number of times per day we say 'fantastic opportunity' to clients	Parentless child
Par	Paragraph	Thing the agency feels below on Monday mornings	Barely acceptable score in golf
Point	Measure of type size	Contribution to debate	Look, over there!

Term	Media meaning	PR meaning	Client meaning
Proof	Copy of made-up page for correction	What the lawyers will demand before allowing any potential libel (q.v.)	Measure of alcoholic potency
Rate card	Price list for advertising space	Clear sign that efforts to procure free publicity for client are not going well	Amusing chap in Yorkshire
Scoop	Exclusive story obtained by outstanding investigative journalism	Story we gave them before anyone else	Implement for serving ice cream
Screamer	Sensational headline	Irritatingly over-emotional colleague	Not what you want in a PA
Serif	Type adornment	Popular Egyptian actor	American law enforcement officer
Spike	Decide not to publish a story	We persuaded them not to run it	The really odd one out of the Goon Show
Splash	The main story on a newspaper's front page	The sound made by a PR who has failed to secure the promised front page coverage taking the easy way out	The glorious meeting of ice cube and gin

Term	Media meaning	PR meaning	Client meaning
Stone	Printers' composing room	Remove seed from fruit	Imperial measure of weight
Stringer	Part-time correspondent	Interviewee who has no intention of accepting a job	Worker on kite assembly line
Sub	Sub-editor, improver of raw copy	Loan from petty cash	U-boat
Syndicated	Appearing in more than one title	Great wheeze for generating lots of coverage	Large and probably rather dodgy loan
Tabloid	Smaller size of newspaper	Mass market newspaper	Type of pill
This difficult time	Period after a tragic death	An average day in the office	Annual General Meeting
Typo	Typographical error: a mistake	Excuse offered for cock-up in press release	Siamese chamber pot

A BIT MORE BLUFFING...

Available from all good bookshops

bluffers.com